Fifty Tales from the Kitchen Garden

A Social History of Vegetables

Bill Laws

First published in 2004 by Sutton Publishing

This edition published in 2017 by Albert Bridge Books

Copyright Bill Laws 2017

Introduction

From A for aphrodisiacs and B for biodynamics to C for compost and V for vegetarians, every vegetable has a story to tell. In spite of being a source of insults - swede basher, cabbage head, couch potato - the vegetable world is as full of life, excitement and anecdote as the flower garden.

Vegetables have relieved, and caused, famines. They have played a part in protest movements and been used to wage, and win, wars. Vegetables shaped the world we know, hot housing Europe on a diet of potatoes and America on 'king corn' or maize.

The ranks of enthusiastic kitchen gardeners range from Roman emperors and US presidents to painters, playwrights and fictional characters and include Thomas Jefferson, Claude Monet, George Bernard Shaw, Rudolph Steiner, Lawrence D. Hills as well as P.G. Wodehouse's Lord Emsworth, Beatrix Potter's grumpy Mr McGregor and Popeye.

Vegetables such as garlic, onions and cabbages have been hailed as wonder foods capable of turbo charging our health and combating cancer. And while one cleric claimed to have calmed the streets of his troubled parish through vegetable growing, the Victorian John Ruskin was convinced that labouring in a kitchen garden improved a person's table manners.

 Bill Laws

In Book I we look at the history of the kitchen garden, the gardener, his tools and his troubles. Book II considers some useful - and curious - garden aids from the compost heap to moon gardening while Book III explores the origins of our most popular vegetables. As Book IV celebrates our vegetable bounty and how we learned to preserve them, Book V ponders on some passionate supporters of the kitchen garden including the Spanish doctor who created the world's biggest vegetable garden of love at Villandry.

Bill Laws, author of the best selling *Fifty Plants That Changed the Course of History*, reveals all in *Fifty Tales from the Kitchen Garden*.

Contents

Introduction iii

Book I - The Kitchen Garden 1
1. The Origins of the Kitchen Garden 3
2. The New World Trade 10
3. The Kitchen Gardener 16
4. St Fiacre and His Spade 24
5. Hoe and Hook 26
6. How Big is My Garden? 31
7. Under Glass 36
8. Pest Control 42
9. The Scarecrow 46
10. The Slug and Snail War 48
11. Mr Henry Doubleday's Solution 50

Book II - Vegetable Husbandry 55
12. The Potting Shed 57
13. Hedge and Fence 61
14. The Walled Garden 65
15. Blanching 69
16. Muck and magic 70

17. The Compost Heap 75
18. John Innes' Revolutionary Potting Composts 79
19. The Findhorn Secret: Growth and Sensibility 81
20. Rudolph Steiner's Biodynamic Vegetables 84
21. Britain's Kitchen Gardens 89

Book III - Origins and Losses 97
22. A Vegetable Timeline 99
23. Out of the East 103
24. Out of India 111
25. Out of Rome 113
26. Out of America 117
27. Out in the Cold 123
28. What's in a Name 125
29. The Secret of Selling Seeds 128
30. Carl Linnaeus and the Classification of Vegetables 135

Book IV - Vegetable Bounty 141
31. Vegetable Healing 143
32. Popeye The Spinach Man 150
33. The Vegetarian Movement 151
34. To Market 153
35. Traditional Traders 157
36. London's Larder 162
37. Onion Johnnies 164
38. Vegetables Preserved 165
39. The Ice House 170
40. A Vegetable Calendar 171

Book V – Vegetable Passions 175
41. *Tildeling*, *kleingarten* and *ogród dzialkowy* 177
42. The Political Potato 183

43. Veggies - A Class Act 190
44. John Loudon: Victorian Gardener 195
45. War Winning Vegetables 198
46. Dig for Victory 202
47. Vegetable Radicals 206
48. Monstrous Vegetables 210
49. Artists and their Kitchen Gardens 214
50. Villandry 219

Further Reading 221
Acknowledgements 227

Book I - The Kitchen Garden

1. The Origins of the Kitchen Garden

As necessary to the well being of a Palestinian household a thousand years ago as it was to an allotment holder in Poland a century ago, the kitchen garden has a long, if obscure history. Garden history has tended to celebrate the pleasure grounds and paradise plots of the wealthy not least because they are better documented and lasted longer than those of their lesser yeomen. Yet the antiquity of the kitchen garden is incontestable and many lie, like a host of Heligans, in outline awaiting rediscovery.

It did not help that classical writers stayed largely silent on the subject of the vegetable plot. In medieval times there was a lexicon of Latin, French and English names for garden places including *gardinium*, *hortus*, *herbarium*, *viridium*, *virgultum* and *vergier*. There was a *wyrtyard*, or little park, and a *herber*, a small ornamental garden with a lawn of less than one acre. The medieval kitchen garden was a *curtilage*, *leac-garth* or *leac-tun* from the Anglo Saxon for *geard*, *tun* or *zeard* meaning a yard or

3

enclosure - this was the 'backyard' that the Elizabethan settlers carried with them to North America.

The common root for the word *giardino* in Italian, *jardin* in French, and *garten* in German, is the Old English *geard* or *garth*, an enclosed place or yard. The first mention of a ketchyngardyn or kechengardyn in Britain appears to be the Bishop of London's manorial accounts of the 1300s. Up until then Europeans kept silent on the subject. The peasant, footstool of the manorial system and mainstay of the medieval economy, had neither the time, skills nor inclination to record anything about his or her methods of growing for the pot. Yet the talents of the peasant gardener ensured that the pottage, a boiled cauldron of vegetables and, occasionally, meat, kept their families alive.

Early European kitchen gardens were little lifelines, fertile plots dedicated to growing the basic necessities. In villages and hamlets across the continent the kitchen garden hugged the house or stood, encircled by earth banks, ditches and stockades, between the cottages and the fields. On the mirey clays of Burgundy or down on the Somerset levels of western England village gardens were raised up above the flood plain and set upon islands surrounded by drainage dykes and the deep, muddy tracks that marked out their boundaries. Ditches, pools and pig wallows were an intrinsic and practical part of the country scene since they manured the ground and watered the vegetables. Unfortunately they regularly swallowed up the young too. Bernard Hanawalt in *The Ties That Bound* reports that: 'On 29 May 1270 Cicely, aged 2 and a half, went into the yard: a small pig came and tried to take bread from her hand. She fell into a ditch and was drowned'.

Although storable winter staples such as vetches and beans might be sown in strips alongside the orchard where the cutting hay and animal pasture grew, the kitchen garden kept to its

Fifty Tales from the Kitchen Garden

conventional 'quarters'. Quartered by a cross of paths, this four square pattern, edged perhaps with low, clipped hedges of yew, juniper, lavender or dwarf box, was as much part of the kitchen garden scene in ancient Persia as it was to the new Elizabethans of the 1950s growing vegetables in their Surrey suburbs.

Back in Roman times Pliny had already worked out that digging over the 'quarters' of a plot of two thirds of an acre to a depth of three feet (9.1 metres) took eight men a day. But we must wait until 820 before some monk saw fit to commit to parchment the design of a European kitchen garden This was the Benedictine abbey, St Gall in Switzerland where the hortus measured a tenth of an acre and the different esculents were grown in 17.7 feet (5.4 metres) long rectangular beds each 19.6 feet (6 metres) by 4.9 feet (1.5 metres) wide.

The division between the kitchen garden and the ornamental garden was, up until the Middle Ages, vague. The average yeoman's wife would be content to mix a damask rose or two among her coleworts (brassicas) and peas. The rose, brought to northern Europe by soldiers returning from the Crusades, was a useful first aid flower, regularly used to treat coughs, colds, eye infections and, according to the Elizabethan botanist John Gerard (1564–1637), 'staunch bleedings'. The gardener and diarist John Evelyn (1620–1706) noted that he had mingled 'choice flowers, and simples' (simples were medicinal herbs) when laying out his private walled garden at Sayes Court in Deptford during the 1660s.

The monastic foundations, however, tended to create clear boundaries between the cloister garden, the physic garden and the cellarer's garden where vegetables and greens (herbs) grew. The Benedictine orders, the later Cistercians and the Augustinians were as closely wedded to their gardens as they were to their God. Monasteries were centered on the cloistered garth, the patch of grass kept as neat as a golfing green not least because the colour green 'nourishes the eyes and preserves their vision,' as one monk would have it. Close by would be the physic garden filled with medicinal plants such as opium poppies, hemlock, sage, rosemary, mint, thyme and mandrake. The orchard cemetery, a pleasant place for a burial with its air of quiet contemplation and sanctuary, lay beyond the cellarer's garden, a utilitarian kitchen garden run to the very best of their abilities by a grumbling friar or nun.

St Benedict advised his followers to keep an open house for travellers and to tend the sick and needy. The peasant paid a tax, a tithe or tenth of his produce, to the clergy. The tax, taken not only from field crops and animals, but also the produce of the 'foot-dug' garden, supported the local monastery, which served as motel, college, roadside diner, citizen advice bureau and hospital, complete with accident and emergency department. Never sure how many guests might be taking bed and board (the board was literally the supper table) and supping at the monastery that evening, the cellarers needed to keep abreast of the latest developments in the cultivation and storage of their esculents.

A cellarer's garden recreated in the monastic gardens of Shrewsbury and designed by Sylvia Landsberg serves to show what the monk Brother Cadfael might have grown. Cadfael, the fictional creation of author Ellis Peters, was an enthusiastic gardener and herbalist who, like his real ancestors, had gained useful knowledge of the apothecary's art from his travels in the Holy Land. Traditional plots of 3.9 feet (1.2 metre) wide beds were surrounded by 1.9 feet (57 centimetre) paths where coleworts, onions, leeks, leaf beet and broad beans were taken to be eaten green. Nitrogen-restoring legumes were an especially useful crop.

Fifty Tales from the Kitchen Garden

Salad, leek and colewort seedlings grew in the nursery bed while the utilitarian fennel, mint, wormwood and hyssop grew nearby. These last were all good 'strewing' plants for spreading on the floors like some medieval air freshener. Cadfael would also have ensured there was a plentiful supply of flax for linen and bandages and hemp for rope and sacking.

The kitchen garden was well stocked. In the 1500s Thomas Tusser lists no less than 1200 plants for the housewife to grow and, while his records included medicinal plants, plants for strewing and scenting hand water and insecticidal plants to keep away the flies, there were plenty of vegetables for the pot. There were brassicas, usually colewort (a kind of kale) and cabbages for the wealthy; parsley, leeks, leaf beet, parsnips, turnips and skirrets (sweet-tasting edible roots); beans and peas, grown to be dried and eaten during the winter; garlic, chives, the 'common bulb onion' and a 'green-leaved one'. In the salad bed the leaves, seeds or petals of a range of self-seeding annuals such as borage, marigold, rocket, feverfew and poppy made as pretty a posy as they did when used to fill the salad bowl.

Around the beginning of the 1500s when Huguenots fled religious persecution in northern Europe the kitchen gardens of England were revitalised. Many Huguenots had lived in the Low Countries, in places like Flanders where the local gardeners customarily grew and shipped fresh vegetables across the Channel to Britain. Peas imported from Holland were reportedly 'fit dainties for ladies, they come so far, and cost so dear,' complained a Mr Fuller. When the Huguenots themselves sailed for England they brought with them their glass and rope work technologies and their expertise in fruit and vegetable growing. By now herbs and salads, parsley and leaf beet, cucumbers and melons, mint and asparagus (cooked first then eaten cold) were growing happily alongside

 Bill Laws

the onion beds, nursery beds of young plants and beds of medicinal herbs. Beetroot, broad beans, cabbage, lettuce, spinach and turnips, meanwhile, were grown in a system of beds and channels. (The turnip, according to one commentator in 1539, was worth growing since 'it augmenteth the seed of man and provoketh carnal lust.')

When Thomas Hill, under the curious pseudonym Didymus Mountain, wrote *The Gardener's Labyrinth* in 1571, he promised to reveal 'worthy Secretes, about the particular sowing and remouing [removing] of the moste Kitchen Hearbes; with the wittie ordering of other daintie Hearbes, delectable Floures, pleasant Fruites, and fine Rootes, as the like hath not heretofore bin vttered [uttered] of any.' Hill advocated trenched beds, with one foot wide (30 centimetre) trenches on either side to water the beds. (This was not to be confused with the practice of 'trenching' or manuring vegetable beds by digging a deep trench and filling the bottom with manure.)

Well-drained paths were laid to separate the vegetable beds from flower borders filled with useful plants such as marigold, ox eye daisies, carnations and pinks. Intercropping was a useful practise, thought Thomas Hill, with broad beans grown between rows of early salads, dwarf and the later tall peas grown together, and strawberry runners, planted between rows of onions, being left to grow on for harvesting the following year, after the onions had been lifted.

The kitchen garden, like the formal flower garden, was kept neat. Seed was sown in drills rather than broadcast or sown in patches. For the fastidious kitchen gardener there was the practise of quincunx, a method of 'planting in rows, by which the plants in the one row are always opposed to the blanks in the other, so that when a plot of ground is planted in this way, the plants appear in rows in four directions'.

Fifty Tales from the Kitchen Garden

As garden fashions developed, the kitchen garden of the 1700s and 1800s was gradually banished to the back of the house, away from the showy flower borders and hand clipped lawns that were designed to greet the house guest. Out of sight was not out of mind, however. Enthusiastic amateurs such as the English naturalist Reverend Gilbert White (1720–1793), author of the *Natural History and Antiquities of Selborne*, (Selborne was his parish in England's Hampshire) would certainly have shepherded his guests around the vegetable patch so that they might share his pride in the 'four rows of marrow-fat pease' and his worries over the vagaries of the weather: 'Sowed a crop of carrots, parnseps, beets, radishes, lettuce, Leeks, Onions; a small crop of Salsafy; red Cabbage-seed, Dutch parsley & Chardoons. There had been a glut of wet for five weeks, & the Ground was rather too moist; but worked pretty well,' he records in his *Garden Kalendar* (1751–73). He was not to know that the contents of the kitchen garden were about to be changed for ever thanks to the Americans.

2. The New World Trade

As Gilbert White wrote his diary, a controversial botanical English writer John Hill (1714–1775) was composing an ambitious botanical compendium. *The Vegetable System*. Struggling to conceive a time when we, the modern reader, might look back on the efforts of his contemporaries he foresaw a future 'perhaps two thousand centuries hence, when after a vaft [vast] space of renewed Barbarism, arts and powers have seated themselves in the remote America.'

It took less than a century and a half for that nation to become a super power and the process, in terms of the kitchen garden, was already well on the way thanks to the exchange of seeds and plants between two Quakers on either side of the Atlantic. London cloth trader Peter Collinson (1694–1768) and the plain-speaking Pennsylvanian farmer John Bartram (1699–1777), started a correspondence in the 1700s that lasted decades. A mutual passion for new plants saw these 'Brothers of the Spade,' as Collinson put it, barter new seed despite perilous obstacles and the long Atlantic journeys.

Fifty Tales from the Kitchen Garden

For the time being, however, the gardeners' choice of vegetables was based upon what had been passed down from the Persians, Greeks, Romans and Christian academics - universities like Toledo, Cordoba, Bologna and Paris had all furthered the development of vegetables as had the great botanical gardens of Pisa, Padua, Parma and Florence. But the growing two-way trade with America would bring about an unparalleled transformation in the vegetable patch.

In America intercropping and companion planting was a well-established craft in the communal gardens of the Native Americans. Corn (maize) was sown, after due ceremony and respectful rituals, and fertilised with whatever was available locally whether it was fish and wood ash or bat dung from neighbouring caves. Corn was followed by lima and kidney or pinto beans, the beans using the stems of the maize for support. Then it was the turn of the pumpkins, squash and sunflowers (for oil) and Jerusalem artichokes (for their storable tubers).

The ripening of the first cobs of corn was a cause for celebration and the cobs would be baked in the embers of the fire at the Green Corn Festival. Mature cobs from the later crops would be hung in ropes likes strings of onions and stored in the smoky rafters of the Indian lodge.

The early European settlers were suspicious at first of South America's maize, potatoes, tomatoes, peppers and yams and North America's vegetable marrows, squash, pumpkins, Jerusalem artichokes and beans. But once they and their families had been rescued from extinction by these Native American crops, they extolled their vegetable virtues and sent the seed home to Europe. It was put to good use. Indian maize was so nutritious that it was said to be responsible for doubling the population of Spain in the 1700s. The potato did the same for the half starved Irish people: before it was arrested by the

 Bill Laws

outbreak of potato blight the population had risen from three million in 1750 to eight million in 1845.

The Industrial Age saw the kitchen garden undergo more radical reforms. Working men grew essential supplies on their allotments; the 'villa' gardener devoted the bottom of the garden to vegetables while the aristocracy poured thousands of pounds into prestigious and productive fruit and vegetable gardens. Snobbery was rife - even in the kitchen garden. 'Let us begin with the earliest crops (of peas) which the cottagers seldom aims at; but which the gentleman's gardener and the amateur must produce, so as to have them on the table long before poor people think of such a thing,' wrote the Victorian gardener Shirley Hibberd (1825–1890). The cottager, amateur and gentleman's gardener, who was generally a cottager in his spare time anyway and perfectly capable of raising early peas if he chose, might have every conceivable vegetable at his disposal, but he still had to contend with the seasons. The methods taken to defeat the seasons would mark the next significant advance.

In Britain, as the market growers in the vales of Kent and Evesham concentrated on mass production, research and development fell to those earnest amateurs on their country estates, aided by armies of gardeners. It was no use relying on 'Johnny Foreigner': 'Horticulture has made little progress in Italy. Forcing or prolonging crops is unknown; everything is sown at a certain season, and grows up, ripens, and perishes together. The red and white beet, salsify, scorzonera, chervile, sorrel, onion, schallot, Jerusalem artichoke, are in many parts unknown,' declared John Claudius Loudon (1783–1843: see John Loudon: Victorian Gardener).

It was left to the estate head gardeners to forward vegetable development, exchanging ideas and sharing their knowledge in

Fifty Tales from the Kitchen Garden

popular publications such as *Gardener's Magazine*, *Gardeners' Chronicle* and the *Journal of Horticulture and Cottage Gardening*.

Technological developments in iron and glass making, and the advancing science of the heating engineer, gave the Victorians the means to grown any and every vegetable - and send them to the table at almost any time of year. All that was required was money and manpower. The rumble of canon fire on the fields of Flanders would bring it all to an end. The Duke of Devonshire's four hundred year old estate at Chatsworth in Derbyshire was a case in point. The great house was provisioned by a seven-acre kitchen garden and, by 1905, with almost two acres of glass housing. No less than forty-six gardeners posed for their photograph before the Great Conservatory in 1890. But by 1917 their numbers were halved. Shortly after the end of the First World War the greenhouses were sold off and plans were drawn up to discontinue the kitchen garden altogether. Death duties, labour costs and, finally, the Second World War would see the greengrocer rather than the gardener provisioning these palaces of the Edwardian and Victorian age.

For the rest of the population, however, urbanisation and the industrial age were reducing city gardens to a fraction of their former selves. There was a saccharine nostalgia for old cottage gardens such as those pictured by Helen Allingham (1848–1926: See Artists and their Kitchen Gardens) where radishes and runner beans grew among the roses. Amateur gardeners were still cropping vegetables where they could, on allotments or pinched plots of wasteland. People pined for a real garden.

On the eve of the 1900s a parliamentary reporter and inventor, Ebenezer Howard, gave voice to their aspirations. Living in the country, he pointed out in his heavily capitalised *Garden Cities of Tomorrow* (1902), brought 'Beauty of Nature, Bright Sunshine and Abundance of Water,' but was blighted by 'Lack of Society,

13

 Bill Laws

Trespassers Beware and Deserted Spirit.' In town the benefits of 'Opportunity, High Money Wages and Places of amusement' had to be offset against 'Closing Out of Nature, Foul Air, High Rents, and Slums and Palaces'. The perfect compromise, argued Howard, was a 'garden city,' a place that combined town and country and which boasted 'Beauty of Nature, Social Opportunity, and Fields and Parks of Easy Access, and Homes and gardens'.

Howard, the son of a London shopkeeper, had emigrated to America and become a frontier farmer in the 1870s and later witnessed Chicago rebuilding itself after Great Fire. He had been heavily influenced by his American experiences and his reforming ideas now paved the way for an era of social housing, gardens and vegetable plots for British people.

He was not the first. Benevolent industrialists such as William Lever at Port Sunlight on Merseyside in Liverpool and George Cadbury at Bournville in Birmingham had already provided vegetable allotments with their workers' homes. Now garden towns modelled on Howard's theories were built at Letchworth from 1903 and Welwyn from 1920. Howard's homes, each with a garden and a vegetable plot formed a template for housing estates through the early part of the twentieth century, although after the war-time frenzy of vegetable growing, the vegetable plot began to retreat down the gardens to be supplanted by flower beds and formal lawns. Meanwhile the increasing availability of imported vegetables made store-bought produce cheap and attractive.

However, just as garden writer Stuart Dudley was suggesting in his *Taking the Ache out of Gardening* (1963) that it was 'uneconomical in the accepted meaning of the word to keep the kitchen supplied with vegetables from the garden,' home grown veg started to enjoy a slow revival.

There was a whole-food movement and a rise in vegetarianism in the 1960s. In the 1970s relaxed students raised vegetables

Fifty Tales from the Kitchen Garden

among their cannabis plants on dubious pieces of squatted ground while in between protests, demonstrations and love-ins, their hippy friends took over neglected allotments and grew vegetables to bulk out their frugal meals of brown rice and bacon bits. Then there were fastidious bio-dynamic gardeners and organic growers who, frustrated in their search for pesticide-free produce, also turned to growing their own. City farms, community gardens and social projects that espoused the therapeutic benefits of growing vegetables sprang up and television, which was overtaking gardening as a popular past time, played its own part by creating some improbable gardening celebrities. There was Don Burke and his CTC media company in Australia, which, in the late 1980s ratcheted up a two million audience every Friday night for *Burke's Backyard*. The Australian programme makers were not unaware of Jim Crockett's *Victory Garden*, which had aired on America's Public Broadcasting Service in 1975. When the 63-year-old died of cancer four years on, the genial garden centre owner, Bob Thomson, replaced him. In the UK thousands were already tuning into BBC radio's *Gardeners' Question Time* which had launched in 1947 on the back of the Dig For Victory campaign and, in its day, hosted such horticultural sounding experts as Bill Sowerbutts, Bob Flowerdew, Fred Loades and Pippa Greenwood. Several of their experts crossed over to television when in 1968 the BBC launched *Gardeners' World* presented by the likes of Percy Thrower, a largely self-taught gardener who had worked his way up from pot boy to parks superintendent at Shrewsbury.

3. The Kitchen Gardener

Percy Thrower came over to television audiences as a genial old horticulturalist. The English author Beatrix Potter, however, portrayed the guardian of the garden, Mr McGregor, as a far sterner figure. In *The Tale of Peter Rabbit* the eponymous hero's mother warns: 'Your father had an accident there; he was put in a pie by Mrs McGregor'. The young rabbit comes face to face with the curmudgeonly Mr McGregor after eating lettuces and some French beans. At one point the bearded Mr McGregor endeavours to stamp Peter Rabbit to death.

In the post war years of the Second World War an equally sanguine figure featured in an instructional cartoon column in Britain's *Sunday Express*. This was Adam the Gardener, who, like Mr McGregor, had about him an almost detectable smell of stale pipe smoke, charity shop clothes and underwear that received irregular washing. Both vegetable growers, Adam and Mr McGregor had, as their antecedents, the pre First World War senior garden staff of mansions and manor houses, those churlish servants who would do only what they would do. How did this stereotype arise? And what became of him?

Fifty Tales from the Kitchen Garden

The *hortolanus or gardinarius* was a person of status in medieval Europe. The *hortolanus* administered the monastery gardens, overseeing the workers who tilled the soil, planted the garlic and the beans, grafted the fruit stock and ensured that the cloister garden remained free of moss and weeds. The workers were often lay gardeners for, although the early Benedictines and Cistercians exhorted their brethren to till the soil themselves, believing that hard work and abstinence brought one closer to God, they were also expert at recruiting novices from the nobility. The pious brother, however devout, preferred to pay a layperson to do his digging for him. Outside the monastery walls, meanwhile, people looked after their vegetables plots as and when they could in the evenings and, as religious rules permitted, at weekends.

In the 1500s the prosperity of the Elizabethan age edged across Britain from the southeast to the north and west, and Britons spent their newfound money, as people always will, on smart homes and fine gardens in what the landscape historian W.G. Hoskins described as the Great Rebuilding of Britain. We can assume that women were the mistresses of these gardens. William Fitzherbert noted in his 1534 *The Book of Husbandrie*: 'The beginning of March ... is time for a wife to make her garden'. Although evidence of the woman's role as the kitchen gardener goes largely unrecorded (apart from occasional accounts of women paid as weeding labourers), common sense suggests that the housewife who managed the household would have kept a close eye on the productive vegetable garden. Early garden authors such as Thomas Tusser (1524–1580) - they were all men - suggest that women's work was confined to flowers, herbs and medicinal plants. However in 1617 William Lawson was completing his book, the *Countrie Housewifes Garden*. In it he offered her advice on the kitchen garden, on 'Planting,

Graffing [grafting], and to make Ground good for a rich Orchard' and on the 'Husbandry of Bees, with their several Uses and Annoyances'. Charles Evelyn, son of the garden writer and designer John Evelyn, also acknowledged the woman's role with his *The Lady's Recreation* published in 1717.

By the early 1800s women gardeners were gaining a better profile. When Jane Webb, the daughter of a Birmingham engineer, married the prolific garden writer John Loudon in 1831, she dutifully helped her husband with his books and encyclopaedia. However she also wrote a series of books for women gardeners including *Gardening For Ladies* and *The Ladies' Flower-Garden* and edited *The Ladies' Companion*, which was founded in 1849. Her husband, 24 years her senior, made little concession to the role of the woman in the kitchen garden. A labourer's garden, he wrote for example, should be large enough to occupy the man in digging and planting and those of 'the female part of the family' or the 'wife and children in hoeing, weeding and watering'. It echoed the attitude of the times epitomised by the King of Sweden's alleged aside to his wife: 'Madam, I married you to give me children, not to give me advice'.

Times were changing. In the States Helena Rutherford Ely, (1858–1920) had published her *A Woman's Hardy Garden* (1903) and Louisa Boyd Yeoman (1863–1948) *The Well-considered Garden* (1915). In 1913 women suffragettes in London attacked the clubby men's world of the garden in their campaign for votes for women by destroying plants in the orchid house at the Royal Botanic Gardens in Kew. Fifteen years earlier the heiress Ellen Willmott, who would die penniless having spent her inherited fortune on her garden at Great Warley in Essex, was awarded the coveted Royal Horticultural Society's Victorian Medal of Honour for her horticultural work. She shared her award (60 medals were awarded in 1897; 58 went to men) with 'the rather

Fifty Tales from the Kitchen Garden

fat, and rather grumbly' Gertrude Jekyll, who herself managed a substantial kitchen garden at her home in Munstead Wood, Surrey. The description of Miss Jekyll came from another woman gardener who would become a significant voice in the gardening world, Victoria Sackville-West.

However, although Gertrude Jekyll and Ellen Willmott both had a reputation for hands-on gardening, their most useful gardening tool was the jobbing gardener himself. Ellen Willmott employed over a hundred of them at her garden, Warley Place. It was the jobbing gardeners who were 'grubbing weeds from gravel paths' in the kitchen garden, as Rudyard Kipling put it in his poem *The Glory of the Garden* (1911). Cheap, and good at all those back-breaking jobs such as manuring, digging and weeding the vegetable plot, the jobbing gardener was also the ideal instrument for planting out and protecting tender seedlings, and harvesting and storing crops.

Jobbing gardeners, like lighthouse keepers and clergymen, were a curious and sometimes eccentric breed. Too isolated by their livelihoods to be supported by an influential trade union movement, their pay traditionally hovered just below the agricultural wage. They were often illiterate. Richard Payne Knight (1750–1824), a scholar who made a name for himself after publicly attacking the society gardener Capability Brown's landscape style, ran his estate at Downton, Herefordshire with the aid of gardener who 'is an extremely simple labourer. He does not know a letter or a figure.'

When things went wrong in the garden, the jobbing gardener could, and usually did, take the blame: 'If those who have private gardens were a little more difficult to please in selecting a gardener, and in the quality of the produce sent to table, the consequences would be an improvement in that produce, and more scientific gardeners,' insisted a haughty Mr Loudon.

However, although most paid gardeners were content with their rank and servitude one or two broke through the glass class ceiling to become men of status and influence. When the bachelor gardener William Robinson died in 1935, he left a 360-acre estate, including an acre of kitchen garden, and the Elizabethan manor house of Gravetye in Sussex. He was the wealthiest garden writer of his time yet began his working life as a garden boy at Curraghmore in Ireland. By 21 he had risen to the rank of foreman in charge of the precious glasshouses on an estate in County Laois. Said to have abandoned his hothouse charges in the middle of the night, the windows open and the fires extinguished, after an argument with the owner, Robinson set off to Dublin to find a new post. It was a good story, if an unlikely one, for he was soon placed with the prestigious Royal Botanic Society in London's Regents Park and began contributing articles to *The Gardener's Chronicle*. *The Times* sent him to Paris as their horticultural correspondent and by 1868 he had published his first book, *Gleanings from French Gardens*. The once poor, apprentice gardener never looked back. He set up a magazine, *The Garden*, in 1875 recruiting that other influential writer, Gertrude Jekyll who would herself edit the magazine at the century's turn in 1899. *The Garden* was sold and merged with *House and Gardens* in 1927. Robinson had already founded another magazine, *Gardening Illustrated*, aimed at the up and coming middle-class suburban and villa gardener. By now the gardener turned publisher was employing his own army of gardeners when he bought Gravetye Manor. His relations with his gardening staff and head gardener Ernest Markham were said to be good. (When he died his last wish, to be cremated, was fulfilled: he had been an early campaigner for incineration rather than burial.)

In Robinson's day the gardener's craft was passed down from generation to generation. When the late George Watkins,

Fifty Tales from the Kitchen Garden

a former head gardener on a Shropshire estate, started work in the early 1900s, his education was a hand-me-down affair: 'I worked under a very clever gardener, George Crew. He had a wonderful way of teaching. He'd give me some packets of seed then he'd keep an eye on me, like, and I got to grow those seeds on, potting on and that sort of thing. With this coaching, he never did anything without he told me what he was doing and the why and the wherefore.'

As a boy, the gardener-to-be would join the house staff as pot washer and apprentice, spending a year or so in the kitchen garden on menial tasks, before moving to spend another year or two on the flower borders. An ambitious young gardener might move on to be a journeyman, settling at other gardens for a period before moving on to better himself. In this way he would hone his skills and widen his knowledge until he could apply for his first post as foreman at a large garden or head gardener at a smaller establishment.

In an era when it was fashionable to keep a fine garden, but unfashionable to get the earth beneath one's nails, the position of head gardener was a potentially prestigious one. But for most who maintained the nation's gardens and grew the household's vegetables, their social ranking 'below stairs' was relatively low. 'You had to touch your cap to all these toffs, you see,' recalled George Watkins.

Nevertheless there were some privileges. Watkins remembered: 'When I was a boy starting in the gardens, gardeners worked until four o'clock on a Saturday, but farm [labourers] till five or six. In 1920, 1921, when I was in Yorkshire, I didn't have to work after twelve o'clock on a Saturday. That was strange to me.' When he moved to Shropshire his Saturday afternoons remained garden-free because the local squire who employed him had a passion for village cricket. 'Sir Henry

 Bill Laws

Ripley, he'd got a great Daimler tourer that could take all of us - the whole team: that was how keen he was on village cricket.'

Generally, however, social class dictated that the gardener and his lordship were not seen in society together. While the gardener might carry on undisturbed in the vegetable plot he kept a low and deferential profile in the rest of the garden. If guests were about he discreetly moved to a different part of the estate.

The kitchen gardener was a necessary nuisance. The mistress of the house had to produce a good table of vegetables and the key to production was her kitchen garden staff: friction between the mistress of the house and the kitchen gardener could have serious consequences. In fiction P.G. Woodehouse's Lord Emsworth was continually frustrated by his head gardener, McAllister. Fact is stranger than fiction: one head gardener recalled how, every year, a neighbouring head gardener on a large estate in the English Midlands would receive a tray of young lettuce seedlings, raised with love and care by his mistress. Just as regularly the vengeful gardener would made sure the plants caught a late frost or were taken by slugs, informing his mistress that her plants had failed once again because the local ground was not good enough for them.

One commentator in the 1800s, John Latouche, condemned the dictatorial ways of the obstinate gardener: 'Have you no spirit left that you submit to be dictated to by a servant?' he demanded. Occasionally the owner made her displeasure public. Baroness Rolle of Bicton in Devon did so of her head gardener, James Barnes, in the 1860s, telling friends that when he left her service, he had abandoned Bicton in a disordered state. Barnes sued the Honourable Baroness for libel, winning the case in 1869 and receiving the equivalent of two years pay, £200, in compensation.

It seems that the grim Mr McGregor, the dour Adam and the intractable McAllister owe their reputations to these stern Edwardian and Victorian gardeners.

4. St Fiacre and His Spade

Not normally a day of special celebration, September 1 is, nevertheless, the feast day of the patron saint of the spade, Saint Fiacre. In the 600s Fiacre left his native Ireland for France where he was welcomed by the Burgundian-born Bishop Faro of Meaux. Faro gave Fiacre a piece of land to found a monastery near what is now Saint-Fiacre-en-Brie. But he imposed one troublesome condition: the monastery could occupy only so much land as could be dug by one man in one day.

Fiacre himself took up the challenge with his trusty spade and when the sun had set Fiacre had turned the sod of no less than nine acres. A hermitage was founded on the site and women were strictly excluded. Even after Fiacre's death any that trespassed were said to suffer mysterious misfortunes.

Fiacre, nevertheless, was destined for sainthood. His reputation as a gardener and a grower of fine vegetables was eclipsed only by his phenomenal powers for curing haemorrhoids. His chapel and shrine remained at Meaux along with his emblem, the spade. (His memory was also enshrined by Parisian cab drivers. When the four-wheeled cabs first appeared for hire in the French capital close by the Hôtel Saint-Fiacre, they were known as *fiacre*.)

Fifty Tales from the Kitchen Garden

Irish links with the spade have continued down the ages. Gangs of Irish 'inland navigators' or navvies formed the backbone of the men who built canals and railways in Britain and Europe. They worked with the same basic hand tool as Saint Fiacre, although it was hand crafted to their own designs. By the late 19th century the craft had developed into one of local distinctiveness as the men of the Ulster spade mills made spades to meet the specific demands of local soils and local traditions. They manufactured more than a hundred different types from the thin, bladed 'loys' of the south and west of Ireland to the dependable two-shouldered Ulster digging spade. There were mud spades and drain spades, trench spades and *slanes* for cutting peat, each fitted with a fine ash handle.

The forerunner of the spade was a very down to earth implement, the mattock or, in Ireland, the *matóg*. The mattock was spade, hoe, trencher and root digger. A close relative of the adze, the house builder's axe used to fashion green and unseasoned oak into house beams, and the butcher's pole axe, the mattock had a broad blade at the one end of the head and a blunt point at the other. As metal technology improved, the garden fork, hand trowel, four pronged fork and hoe, tended to push the mattock to the back of the tool shed although it continues to serve rural communities across the globe today.

5. Hoe and Hook

The best way to weed the vegetables patch, according to William Fitzherbert writing in his *The Book of Husbandrie* was with a hoe or a forked stick and a hook 'ground sharpe both behind and before'. The thorny problem of clearing virgin ground, meanwhile, was solved with a hook or bill hook. The design of the hook, like that of any other tool prior to the Industrial Revolution, varied from region to region, even from parish to parish. In England alone more than 25 designs have been recorded for hedge making, pruning and cutting back and harvesting stakes and poles from the woods: 'by hook and by crook' was the legal term for working the manor woods.

    The bill hook's smaller brother, the sickle, was a harvesting tool, handy for topping large quantities of carrot or beet before they were put to store in sand or peat, and for clearing paths around fruit trees. Down the years a favourite sickle would come to resemble the cusp of a new moon through its razor-edged blade being honed so often upon the sharpening stone.

    The billhook's big brother, the scythe, came into its own in the autumn for mowing the long meadow or orchard grass. In times of trouble and political unrest, during the English Peasants' Revolt of 1381 for example, all four (mattock, scythe, sickle and hook) were appropriated from the tool store and born as lethal weapons for close combat fighting. The close cousin of the scythe, the *fauchard* or military scythe was taken into battle in the late 1780s by the rebel leader Tadeusz Kościuszko (1746–1817) as he led his fellow Polish fighters on a doomed attempt to wrestle the country back from Russian rule. The scythe's strategic significance in hand to hand fighting was considered by the Polish architect Chrystian Piotr Aigner (1756–1841) in his *Brief Treatise on Scythes and Pikes*. History would repeat itself when home guardsmen, short of weaponry, once again raided the garden tool shed during the Second World War.

The garden diarist John Evelyn pictured a basic set of garden tools in his *Elysium Britannicum*, which he began in the 1650s. His pen drawings show a conventional range of tools including wooden sieves for sifting potting soil, seed sowing boxes, dibbers and wooden rakes lined with timber teeth. Those 'wedge(d) with oke' were the superior sort. If Evelyn were to journey forward in time for three and half centuries he might be amused to find the hoe, rake, hook and shears of his age still in use even if he would be confounded by the quantity of plastics used in the contemporary kitchen garden.

The beginnings of the Industrial Revolution marked the start of mass marketing in the kitchen garden tool trade. During her 64-year-tenure of the British throne, Queen Victoria (1819–1901) ruled a quarter of the globe and one in four of every person upon it. Her servants gardened in far flung corners of the empire: 'Your Le Floral is the most remarkable stuff,' wrote one of her Indian army sergeant-majors, Mr J. Binns from Pachmarhi, Central Provinces, East India to Sutton's seeds in 1837. Sutton's was then branded as 'seedsmen to His Imperial Majesty the German Emperor,' a company, which in common with garden

 Bill Laws

tool manufacturers, offered 'carriage paid to all the principal ports in England when orders amount to 60s'.

Victoria's reign witnessed the transformation of the kitchen garden and the tools that turned it. In 1851 her husband Prince Albert organised The Great Exhibition at the Crystal Palace in London. More than 100,000 exhibits were displayed including the very latest in kitchen garden technology (together with Sam Colt and his patented Colt Navy revolver and Mathew Brady who would shortly achieve fame with his daguerreotypes of the American civil war). One gardener who attended the Great Exhibition, but then refused to go inside because he disapproved of the 'ugly' exhibits was the eighteen-year-old William Morris. Morris believed the Exhibition had been hijacked by the nation's industrialists and used as a vehicle to promote mass production. Morris would go on to revive the craft of natural vegetable dyeing while his Arts and Crafts movement encompassed garden design, espousing the cause of the Romantic medieval garden and its handsome hand tools.

Six million people with money to spend attended the Great Exhibition. Their tool stores were soon filled with every conceivable horticultural device. Sutton, for example, could offer a choice of three dozen garden penknives including a special asparagus knife, Ladies budding Knife, Pruning Knife and Saw ('Superior') and Knife with two blades and a botanical lens. There were seven different spades and 22 different hoes; five 'Improved Garden Engines' (wheeled water barrels) and eight wheelbarrows with a choice of wooden or iron wheels; and no less than 28 different carts for moving manure.

A century later, and in the aftermath of such radical social change that a veritable army of jobbing gardeners had disappeared, kitchen garden tool sheds were full of dusty relics. Some were profitably tidied away with the latest American invention, the shadowboard, which offered a proper place for every tool. Most, however, were scrapped and replaced by inferior steel and plastic substitutes. In the post war period new tools for the kitchen garden were designed to help the single-handed owner gardener to manage on his or her own. The ubiquitous mechanical tiller, which stormed through the backyards of America, had been invented by a Swiss gardener based on his observations of a dog digging for a bone. Meanwhile wheeled hoes and powered ploughs, steel wheel barrows and chain saws, strimmers and chuntering motor mowers flooded the market - Sunday mornings could never be quiet again.

Innovations included hopeless failures such as the hand weeding glove of 1965, which dripped with weed killer and was used to stroke offending weeds to death, and spectacular successes like the Flymo for gliding over grassy paths between the vegetable beds, and Gro-bags which allowed people with no garden to grow a small crop of vegetables.

Nevertheless certain kitchen garden hand tools did stand the test of time. They included the hand-trowel and the French secateurs. The latter had been developed by a French count, Antoine François Bertrand de Molleville (1744–1818), in the early 1800s. Molleville's device employed two sharpened blades that clipped with a pincer-like action, a design he considered ideal for use in the vineyards.

The English were not alone in preferring a good knife. Penknives, so named from being used to trim quills or 'pens,' were turned out by the dozen by local blacksmiths until mass manufacturers cornered the trade. One Savoyard brand was inadvertently promoted across France by local railwaymen employed by the Paris, Lyon and Mediterranean Rail company. These were the rail men who, based at Chambéry, always bought their pocket knives from Joseph Opinel. He had started making

Bill Laws

knives in 1890 and the Opinel with its hardened Swedish steel blade, safety steel ring (a feature added in the 1950s) and wooden handle, soon became a favourite amongst French gardeners. (It also appealed to mountaineers: in 1959 an alpinist called Pierre Paquet claimed to have cut himself free from his snow tomb in an avalanche with his Opinel.)

A successful rival, the *Schweizer Offiziersmesser*, came out a year after the Opinel. Supplied to the Swiss army, the knife not only opened steel cans, but its additional tools could be used to dismantle a standard-issue army rifle. It was said that US army soldiers, stumbling over the problems of German pronunciation, dubbed it the Swiss army knife.

The garden writer John Loudon favoured not the knife, but the secateurs, which he thought, were 'particularly adapted for lady gardeners'. He counselled his countrymen to set aside any anti-European sentiment and adopt them: 'I know well the prejudice that exists in England among horticulturists against this kind of thing, and their almost superstitious regard for a good knife.'

6. How Big is My Garden?

Accurate measurement is an essential tool in the vegetable garden. It always was. Early Frankish law, for example, dictated that, for the purposes of legal compensation, an orchard must consist of at least 12 trees in an enclosure 60 feet (18.2 metres) by 80 feet (24.3 metres). The garden writer Shirley Hibberd specified in the late 1800s: 'The Brazil beet requires eighteen inches; and the plants a foot and a half asunder for the crop sown in April.' Similarly one wartime garden guide directed: 'Cabbage. Sow thinly 1 inch deep. As soon as the plants have made four or five leaves they should be planted out from 24 inches apart.'

With her husband away fighting, this Second World War-time West Midlands housewife was determined to dig for victory to supplement her family's rations. 'I dug up the front lawn and learned to grow vegetables from my neighbour. He was an old man and he always used a tape measure not only between the rows and between the plants too.'

The desire for accuracy in the vegetable beds could become an obsession and we must temporarily abandon the metric system to better appreciate it. The West Midlands veteran gardener relied on the Imperial system, in use in Britain for 600 years until the British Parliament voted to go metric in 1963. America's customary system, like the measurings of the Liberians and Myanmar, resisted the lure of metrification and remained firmly rooted in the foot and inches camp where the principle unit of measurement was the human body. The recommended dimensions for the average American vegetable bed, for example, was 16 feet (4.8 metres) by 10 feet (3 metres) or four feet square (1.2 metres) for small raised beds.

Horses are still measured in 'hands,' people still 'pace' out their plots and sow with a 'pinch' of seeds. A foot, a step and an arm span were useful measures in the Middle Ages when the English King Henry 1 legalised his 'imperial' measure of the foot and the yard (three feet), which was based on the distance between the tip of the Royal nose and the thumb of his outstretched arm. Before he died in 1135, an Iron Yard of Our Lord King was lodged in London and exact copies, cast in bronze or brass, were delivered throughout the kingdom.

Yet 5,000 years ago when the boundaries surrounding the farms and vegetable gardens along the river Nile were regularly washed away by floods, the Egyptians used a rope of 100 cubits, the cubits marked by knots, to re-establish the garden boundaries. The Royal Cubit was cast from a block of black granite against which every cubit measuring stick was checked for accuracy. The cubit could be subdivided into 28 'digits' and the success of the system can be measured against the pyramids, built with these measurements.

In China the traditional unit of measure, the chi, dating back to the first dynasty possibly 2,000 years ago, was .82 inches (25 centimetres) long and based on the distance between the pulse and the base of the thumb. Ten chi made a zhang, approximately 11.4 feet (3.5 metres).

Fifty Tales from the Kitchen Garden

In the Middle East, however, as power and influence swung away from Egypt and into the Mediterranean, it was the turn of the Greeks who, still using a variant on the finger, adapted the Egyptian cubit to equal 24 fingers. They made their basic unit of length one foot or 16 fingers and when it was the Rome's turn to set a global standard, they too used the foot, but sub divided it into *uncia* or twelfths. Longer lengths were measured as a pace, which was two steps, one with the left foot, one with the right and a thousand paces made a *mille,* or a mile.

A foot, a step or an arm span were still useful garden measures in the Middle Ages. While merchants measured their wool in *ells,* the distance between the elbow and the fingertip, and the Vikings measured a fathom as so many lengths of a sailor's arm, the mediaeval vegetable garden was measured in feet. A standard size, measured with an 84 foot (25.6 metre) cord on a triangulation of 3:4:5 (21 feet - 6.4 metres, 28 feet – 8.53 metres and 35 feet – 10.6 metres) produced an accurate vegetable plot 28 foot (8.53 metres) long and 21 foot (6.4 metres) wide. The plot could be divided into four or five strips, narrow enough to allow the bed to be cultivated without the gardener walking across it and compacting the soil. 'Beds should be so contrived that the hands of those who weed them may easily reach the middle of their breadth, so that those who are weeding may not be forced to tread on seedlings, to the help of which let the paths be of such a width (as a man's foot) that they may weed first one half and then the other half of the bed,' advised Thomas Hill very sensibly in 1577.

Larger garden areas occurred in the village 'clos' (in Scandinavian the 'toft') a strip of ground at the rear of the cottage, measuring between 30 foot (9.1 metres) and 60 foot (18.2 metres) wide and 200 (60.9 metres) to 600 feet (182.8 metres) long. Although part of the patch would be put down to pasture and orchard and part devoted to those wonder materials of the medieval age, flax or hemp, a significant area would be dug by foot ready for planting the *worts* or plants. The furlong, an eighth of a mile and based on the distance a horse could plough without needing to pause for a rest, was more of an agricultural measure, but the acre, representing a patch of ground which a team of oxen could plough in a day, was, and still is, used for larger gardens. The acre measured 4840 square yards (4425.6 square metres) and could be sub divided into 160 *perches*, from the Latin pole or staff. (Measuring the feet of the first sixteen parishioners leaving the church on a Sunday was judged a sound method of establishing a perch.)

Apart from the addition of the 22-yard long 'chain' introduced by Edmund Gunter (1581–1626), an English astronomer and mathematician whose surveyor's chain is still used in American agriculture, the Imperial system served the vegetable gardeners of England unchallenged until 1791.

Then in post-revolutionary France, a committee of the French Academy of Science defined a new, revolutionary unit of measurement, the metre, so called after the Greek word, metron, or measure. Before metrication the French gardener managed with twelve *lignes* to a *pouce* (inch), twelve *pouces* to a *pied* (foot) and six *pieds* to a *toise* (just under two metres). Now, according to the Academy, the system was to be based on multiples of ten and the basic unit, the metre, on one ten millionth of the distance between the Equator and the North Pole. The Academy did not have the means to actually measure that distance and had to base their calculations instead on the findings of two French surveyors who calculated it after measuring the more manageable distance between Dunkirk and Barcelona.

Once the new metric system had been adopted, the Gallic equivalent of Egypt's granite cubit was cast in a platinum alloy and stored at the weights and measures bureau in Sèvres. A miscalculation meant that the world's first metre fell slightly shorter: the error was ignored and plaques demonstrating the standard measure were put up in town halls across France.

The metric system, when it was introduced to the United States over a century ago, was largely ignored by gardeners. And after more than half a century of metrication in British gardens, there remained a marked reluctance amongst gardeners to use anything other than King Henry's imperial standard. Despite the advent of the automobile and computerised algorithms, allotment dimensions continued to be based on measurements from the Middle Ages: section 22 of the Allotments Act 1922 described an allotment garden as 'not exceeding forty poles in extent'.

7. Under Glass

In some parts of the Dutch lowlands the sight of naked soil is a rarity. Instead a sea of glass covers the polders and protects acres of vegetables ripening under all the advantages of free solar power. In the new mechanised age of gardening, the Dutch glasshouses hum with computer-controlled hydroponics feeding soil-free tomatoes, cucumbers and bell peppers. Not for nothing were glass-covered vegetable frames, or Dutch lights, so named.

Just under four centuries ago, the gardener diarist John Evelyn explained his own method of harnessing natural energy to grow plants. He was delivering his *Philosphical Discourse on Earth* to the Royal Society, an organisation established by the English king, Charles II, and devoted to promoting the arts and sciences. Evelyn explained how forcing pits, deep enough for a man to stand in, should be filled with steaming dung, hot with aerobic activity. Plants grown on in portable wooden trays and placed over the pits, he explained, would positively thrive with this natural bottom heat.

Shirley Hibberd in his *Profitable Gardening* also gave the forcing pit a vote of approval: 'In times gone by there was nothing better than the hot house frame or pit, heated with leaves and stable manure, and in skilful hands there was generally no

Fifty Tales from the Kitchen Garden

difficulty in obtaining plenty of fruit'. But, he warned, 'the dung-frame was very uncertain of productiveness'.

Evelyn and his *Discourse* helped to promote the 'green house' and the 'conservatory,' both places where gardeners could conserve their green plants over winter. Early experimenters used wood, stone and brick to create greenhouses, but by 1697 the Duke of Devonshire commissioned for his stately home in the English Peak District, Chatsworth, one of the early glass greenhouses. By now designers had come to realise that ventilation was vital, that the reflective quality of whitewashed walls would raise the temperature inside, and that a glass roof set at a slope of precisely 52 degrees maximised the effects of the sun, which, at midday, struck the glass at right angles.

Such technical developments were spurred on by a mania for growing tender plants especially the pine or pineapple, and by a 19th century passion for public and private winter gardens. (It was also boosted in Britain in the 1840s by the repeal of a prohibitive tax on glass.) The 295 foot (90 metre) long Jardin d'Hiver in Paris' Champs Elysées rose up almost three stories high in 1847 while a vine house at Buffalo in the US housed over 200 vines in its 689 feet (210 metre) length. Some years earlier in 1832 the Duke of Devonshire had taken on an enthusiastic young man called Joseph Paxton as head gardener at Chatsworth. Paxton was responsible for a new glasshouse, designed by Decimus Burton and christened with typical Victorian hyperbole as the Great Conservatory. It occupied an acre (0.5 ha) of ground, was heated by over six miles (9.5 km) of iron heating pipes and the entrance was so wide that, visiting in 1843, Queen Victoria could be driven by carriage straight into the building.

A year later work started on architect Decimus Burton's design for a palm house at Kew's Royal Botanical Gardens near London. Covered with 16,000 panes of glass the structure resembled the upturned hull of a giant steamship (the technology for the wrought iron work came from the Thames' ship yards). One of plants that failed to thrive at Kew was an Amazonian lily, the Victoria regia. It was transferred to Chatsworth where Paxton set about designing a special lily house. He had noted the remarkable carrying capacity of the lily's giant leaves (he found that a single floating leaf could support the weight of his young daughter Alice) and it inspired him to produce a ridge and furrow design for the wrought iron work. The lily house complete (and the lily having flowered) Paxton now sketched out a design employing his narrow, wrought-iron bars for a new glass building. His initial sketch, on an old sheet of blotting paper, would be turned into the largest and most prestigious glass house of the time. The satirical magazine Punch dubbed it the Crystal Palace and when it was completed at Hyde Park, London in 1851 it housed the Great Exhibition.

These glass houses impressed the merchants, bankers and industrialists of the age, and the villa conservatory and green houses became an aspirational addition to any house of status. Shirley Hibberd regarded such structures as things of beauty. 'A houseful of melons or cucumbers, showing a rich screen of foliage between the eye and the sun, and the fruits hanging below it, as they would naturally if the plants were twining among the trees of their native soils, is one of the finest sights in the whole range of horticultural exhibitions.'

Technical advances in glass making powered the popular development of the green house. In the early 1800s broad or cylinder glass had first to be blown into a cylinder and then opened out flat and cut into sheets or panes. Plate glass, where molten glass was poured out onto a casting table and then laboriously ground and polished smooth was introduced in the late 1800s. Both were expensive for horticultural use. The alternative was

Fifty Tales from the Kitchen Garden

crown glass, which was spun into a large disc and then cut into squares and diamonds, the thickened bull's eye centre being thrown back into the furnace (or sold on to publicans who had to constantly repair windows broken by their boozy revellers).

John Loudon condemned 'economy, as to the quality of glass,' declaring it as self defeating since it resulted in 'the sickly pale etiolated appearance of plants more painful than agreeable to the eye of any who take an interest in the vegetable kingdom'. Despite the expense, the late 19th century witnessed a frenzy of green house building on a more modest scale. There were great, double span cucumber houses and meloneries, genteel plant preservers and what one manufacturer described as 'lawn conservatories invaluable for the use of Amateurs in the forwarding of various seeds'. There were pit frames and lean-to greenhouses, and glazed forcing houses calculated to 'convince all practical minds of the importance and utility of this class of House for Gentlemen, Nurserymen, Market Gardeners, and, in fact, all those who require a cheap, strong House for Forcing, or growing Cucumbers, Tomatoes, Melons.'

Away from the glass house, gardeners rich and poor took advantage of cold frames and the French *cloche,* originally a bell-shaped glass (hence its name), to bring on early vegetables or shelter late crops from the frost.

Inside the greenhouse, meanwhile, a variety of heating systems were tried out from pits of tan bark (sheets of oak used in the tanning industry), which with controlled anaerobic activity could achieve temperatures of up to 42 degrees centigrade, to smokey boilers that burned anthracite, charcoal or coke and sent streams of hot water rushing along a circuitry of cast iron pipes buried beneath the growing beds. Such methods had been trialled as far back as 1750 and by the late 1800s there was even a device invented that would rouse the under gardener from his bed in the middle of the night, should the temperature fall too low. The clarion call of the fire alarm, however, was a relatively late development - the Massachusetts inventor Francis Robbins Upton was still working on what was incorrectly registered at the patent office as a tire (fire) alarm in 1890. As a consequence glasshouses were frequently destroyed by accidental fire.

The benefits gained of a little 'bottom heat,' heating the soil from below, had been familiar to gardeners for centuries. The Moor horticulturalist Ibn Bassal created a royal garden for Al-Mu'tamid (1040–1095; Al-Mu'tamid was a noted Andalusian poet and the last caliph of Seville in Spain) and wrote a treatise on soil fertility. In exploring the methods of preparing the soil he gave detailed instruction on how to raise early seedlings with natural 'bottom heat'. Initially a dung heap of slightly-dried mule dung, pepped up with a dash of pigeon dung, was built. Seeds were then sown on top in a compost of dry-dung and sheltered from the elements with cabbage leaves. Germination was speeded up by the natural warmth from beneath and the heap could maintain a steady anaerobic heat for up to five weeks provided it was kept under constant supervision: a dung bed that overheated would cook rather than cultivate young plants.

A thousand years later the more reliable method of steam pipes, laid like a domestic heating system had taken over in the great glasshouses. But the expense was unsustainable. Every winter the Great Conservatory at Chatsworth burned 300 tons of coal. Wartime coal shortages during the First World War saw it demolished in 1920 along with other great glass houses across Europe. In the future lay computer controlled, solar-aided electrical and gas heating systems.

Yet in some country homes in the 1920s the greenhouse still played a central role in servicing the manor house and its guests. The Shropshire lad, George Watkins, looked back on

Fifty Tales from the Kitchen Garden

his days as a head gardener during the period: 'Between the front of the house and the servant's quarters at the back, you had the old green baize door. There's a bell there to ring Madam. You'd go in about ten o'clock in the morning to meet The Lady in the kitchen and discuss what vegetables she'd like. You got to try and get about three [different] vegetables a day and you couldn't put the same three vegetables in on the run so you got to get so many varieties to follow on all the year round.

'We ran a big conservatory and a heated greenhouse. Heating was so cheap in those days a truck-load of anthracite would be enough to keep you going for the winter. In the conservatory side was vines, then you got to grow carnations, chrysanths [chrysanthemums], cinerarias and cyclamen for The Lady. Off that [conservatory] again you'd got a plant house where you forced potatoes and beans and tomatoes and cucumbers and anything like that. We used to force dwarf beans, salsify, carrots, beetroots and celeriac. You name it, we got it.'

8. Pest Control

Once upon a time people grew vegetables because without them their families would perish. That once-upon-a-time covered some of the bleakest periods in world history from plagues and pestilences to genocidal wars. In the new millennium, however, many people took up the craft of growing vegetables in kitchen gardens and allotments simply to avoid poisoning their families. The US Department of Agriculture had reported pesticide residues on 73% of the foods they examined at one point in the 1990s and while the food industry insisted that contamination levels were perfectly safe, consumers felt less confident over the reassurances. Jude Cooper had held an allotment in the Welsh border town of Hay-on-Wye for 30 years. 'Growing our own vegetables is a form of rest and relaxation and there's a great spirit of camaraderie on the allotments: but above all I can eat what I know - and I know what I grow is free of potentially carcinogenic pesticides'.

    A century earlier some of the more powerful pesticides used to boost productivity came from natural sources, as former head gardener Keith Ruck recalled: 'Nicotine was our main thing for all insecticides, and green sulphur for fungi diseases. You bought nicotine liquid from the chemist or you bought nicotine shreds

Fifty Tales from the Kitchen Garden

for fumigating the greenhouses. These were tobacco leaves cut up and soaked with nicotine to make them extra deadly. You'd put six heaps in the conservatory and light them. By the time you got to light the last it would be getting a bit strong in there.'

There were various ways of dealing with pests outside the glasshouse. In his 1863 *Profitable Gardening* the garden writer Shirley Hibberd advocated using a drench of laurel water to eradicate caterpillars from the brassica tribe. The leaves and fruits of the hedging bush, English or cherry laurel (*Prunus laurocerasus*) contain cyanide-like toxins (they have the characteristic almond smell of cyanide). Laurel leaves have been fatally mistaken for those of the bay tree. Hibberd offered the alternative of hand-picking the caterpillars which was 'very effectual and not so endless a job as it may appear'. He recommended dipping the roots of brassica transplants in a puddle of chimney soot and lime before planting to protect them against club root (a century later gardeners used a solution of disinfectant in the same way) and liked to loose a 'brood of young ducks – the best vermin destroyer' – to clean up the cabbage patch.

In John Loudon's opinion the worst pests in the garden were 'the human enemies... such as break in secretly to steal clandestinely'. He recommended that 'the dog is most effectual,' but also considered 'man-traps, spring-guns, and alarums... have considerable influence'. Like one Middle Ages commentator who declared: 'wormes that... waster my herbes, I dash them to death,' Loudon too waged war on the friendly worm insisting on 'gathering by hand all worms, snails, slugs, grubs, and other insects, as soon as they appear.'

Other products of the 1800s included plant-based powders and sprays derived from the poisonous plants including derris, tobacco, hellebore (an emetic), pyrethrum and quassia. Home made recipes for camphor, soft soap, sulphur and turpentine coped with mealy bugs and white scale while smouldering laurel leaves put paid to green- and whitefly.

A common domestic garden poison was arsenic. It was employed against unwanted pests both inside and outside the garden: in 1922 a Hay-on-Wye solicitor, Major Herbert Armstrong, was hanged for poisoning his wife with arsenic intended for the garden. In America in the 1940s, meanwhile, the tobacco-based Black Leaf 40 was a sure protection against most bugs while mothballs, nicotine sprays and pyrethrum were all allowed to enter the human food chain as they were routinely applied to vegetables. Another handy chemical in the garden shed was calcium cyanide gas, useful for dealing with burrowing woodchucks, chipmunks and rats.

By the end of the Second World War a chemical armoury, developed for commercial market gardeners and vegetable farmers, was filtering down to the back yard gardener. The British Ministry of Agriculture, for example, recommended derris dust as being especially effective with flea beetle. For those who felt uneasy about chemical killing there was a mechanical aid available – the greased flea beetle wheel. This was a home made circle of cardboard, pinned to a cane and plastered with the thick grease normally reserved to lubricate the moving parts of the family automobile. The theory was sound: as the gardener pushed the greased unicycle along a row of affected beetroot the alarmed flea beetle leapt, as only fleas do, struck the card and stuck fast. (I have tried it and cannot recommend it.)

In 1963 the British garden writer Stuart Dudley ('the only good weed is a dead weed') reflected the general view of the post-war vegetable grower in *Taking the Ache out of Gardening*. 'Let it not be said in this jet age of today that the gardeners of England are fighting the Weed War of today with the weapons of Napoleon,' he wrote. 'Our back-room boys have provided the wherewithal

Fifty Tales from the Kitchen Garden

to blot out the whole of the plant and insect kingdom – let us use them with due circumspection.' The implication was clear: the boffins must know what they were doing and the gardener should carry on with the battle, albeit with care.

By the 1960s, however, there were serious signs that horticultural and agricultural chemical warfare was damaging the environment. In his seminal *The Complete Book of Self Sufficiency* (1976), John Seymour offered a practical approach to the recurring, utopian dream of the back-to-the-landers. 'The true homesteader will seek to husband his land, not exploit it,' he wrote. 'He will realize that if he interferes with the chain of life (of which he is a part) he does so at his peril, for he cannot avoid disturbing a natural balance.' The sensitive gardener would 'always get pests and diseases but they will not reach serious proportions,' he wrote, advocating a holistic and essentially benevolent approach to growing vegetables.

9. The Scarecrow

One of the benevolent ways of scaring away avaricious birds was to pay small children to shake a rattle. A cheaper alternative was that perennial bogeyman, the scarecrow. A favourite figure of folklorists and horror film makers, the scarecrow, or the German *vogelscheuche*, the Danish *fugleskræmsel*, the French *épouvantail*, or Scotland's *tattie bogle* (he protected the potatoes or tatties) were all designed to put the wind up the avian world. Some were designed to flap threateningly in the breeze, to offer the menacing profile of a gardener with a gun or to moon at passers-by with a bare, pumpkin bottom peeping over their pants. Some even smelled bad: Japanese gardeners made their *kakashis* additionally offensive by draping bamboo poles with old rags and rotting or burnt offal.

The Roman writer Columella took a belt and braces approach to scaring off vermin and recommended the additional use of placatory sacrifices including the 'blood and entrails of a sucking whelp' or the skinned head of an Arcadian ass to assist the work of the 'night flying birds' which were hung on crosses. Roman and Greek gardeners made the most of another mannequin, the god of the garden Priapus who carried a scythe in one hand, the hopeful token of a good harvest, while exhibiting his oversized phallus, a second symbol of fertility. Centuries later their Latin descendants scared pesky Mediterranean birds away with sun-bleached animal skulls perched on poles.

In popular fiction one of the scarecrow's more sinister manifestations was the character of Dr. Syn, created by writer Russell Thorndyke, brother of the English actress Sybil Thorndyke. Thorndyke's 1915 novel *Doctor Syn* (remade by Walt Disney as *The Scarecrow of Romney Marsh* in 1963) featured the macabre figure of the scholar turned smuggler, Christopher Syn, who roamed the lonely marshes of south-east England disguised as a scarecrow. Dr Syn continues to crop up in the swathe of autumnal scarecrow festivals that have become as commonplace as they are creative. (One myopic British car driver called out the emergency services after witnessing what she took to be an equine accident at the side of the road. It turned out to be a horse-themed tableau, part of the annual Great Doddington Scarecrow Festival.)

10. The Slug and Snail War

Two thousand years of pest control has failed to resolve a problem that has vexed gardeners since kitchen gardening began: slugs and snails. 'Sowed a pint more of dwarf kidney beans in the room of those that were devoured by snails,' wrote a grumpy Gilbert White in 1759. Many garden authors have expressed their own view on controlling these terrestrial molluscs.

    We have already heard Lucius Junius Moderatus Columella's (4AD-70AD) suggestion that the gardener offer a sacrifice of a dead 'sucking whelp'. Equally he could have collected ashes from the public baths and scattered them around vulnerable plants or adopted the strategy of Ibn Bassal who advised laying cabbage leaves around the vegetable plot under which slugs and snails would congregate companionably over night. The early rising gardener could then scoop them up and dispose of them. Other methods of disposal included dropping the creatures into a mixture of ashes and unslaked lime, sprinkling them with quick lime or salt, or feeding them to the family ducks. Alternatively a family of ducklings could be kept for the express purpose of protecting the vegetables. Bartram's London correspondent

Fifty Tales from the Kitchen Garden

Peter Collinson was said to have kept four pet seagulls to do the job at his garden in Peckham.

A variety of infusions were deployed in the slug and snail war including one of walnut leaves, salt and crushed shells, crushed tobacco leaves or a bitter mix of water and vinegar or lime water.

What one commentator referred to as these 'little beasts injurious to kitchen gardens' could be 'annoyed' by surrounding vulnerable plants with prickly barley straw or collars made of zinc or copper. By the 1950s, however, some significantly more effective controls were being marketed: they included mixing metaldehyde, a toxic, organic molluscicide with bran or tea leaves and leaving heaps of the poison around the plot. Its toxicity, however, resulted in several cases of animal and human poisoning. Many gardeners turned instead to the slug trap approach. Lawrence D Hills, founder of the Henry Doubleday Research Association (see later), explained the slug trap to readers of his *Grow Your Own Fruit and Vegetables* in 1971. 'The traditional soup plate, wide and shallow, sunk level with the ground and filled with a mixture of 1 part of beer to 2 of water, sweetened with 1 dessertspoonful of Barbados sugar to 1 pt of the mixture.' Hills, who also advocated keeping a hedgehog to counter the problem, reported capturing 60,000 slugs in one garden in a year.

The squeamish or compassionate gardener could collect slugs and snails by hand and either hurl them over the garden wall into the neighbour's patch or transport them to a different neighbourhood. However, several amateur experiments involving the marking of snails shells with identifying paint suggested the snail had good homing instincts. Perhaps the best advice was that of a live-and-let-live gardener Rick Guest: 'Each evening I go around collecting them by hand and then I return them to where they belong and where they are happy to live - the compost heap'.

11. Mr Henry Doubleday's Solution

In the 1970s, when John Seymour's *The Complete Book of Self Sufficiency* was published, E. F. Schumaker, author of *Small is Beautiful*, voiced the concerns of a new generation in his introduction to Seymour's book. People, he warned were over dependent on fantastic machinery and on larger and larger incomes. 'They may claim to be more highly educated than any generation before them, but the fact remains they cannot really do anything for themselves.' In the vegetable garden, at least, that was about to change.

Britain's Soil Association, founded to promote organic growing, had been set up in 1943 by society girl turned organic farmer, Eve Balfour (1898–1990), after she published her best seller, *The Living Soil*. It promoted the organic cause and influenced the writings of the marine biologist from Southport Island, Maine, Rachel Carson. In its turn her *Silent Spring* (1962) - the title was a reference to what the future held if nations continued to poison their soil with fertilisers and pesticides - helped shape the global environmental movement.

Fifty Tales from the Kitchen Garden

In the 1950s freelance journalist Lawrence Hills had already set himself the novel task of growing vegetables and fruit 'organically'. In pre war dictionaries organic meant 'pertaining to the animal and vegetable worlds; forming a whole with a systematic arrangement of parts.' But now, in the 1960s as Hills explained, 'organic' had become invested with a new and potent meaning. An organic gardener would be one who had given up chemical fertilisers, pesticides and herbicides. 'Some (gardeners) change on ethical grounds to stop pollution harmful to birds, bees and men, others to save money, since it is easy even at today's vegetable prices to spend more on chemicals that you save when growing your own food,' he wrote.

Hills had been intrigued by the horticultural experiments of an obscure 19th century Quaker called Henry Doubleday (1810–1902). In the 1870s Doubleday, who ran a small business producing gum for postage stamps, had experienced difficulties sourcing his usual gum arabic, derived from the acacia tree. When he heard that prickly comfrey (*Symphytum asperum*), a native of the Caucasus, was reputed to contain much 'mucilaginous matter,' and could potentially be a source of gum, he wrote to a gardener at the palace of St. Petersburg in Russia requesting some plants.

The gardener sent Russian comfrey (*Symphytum X uplandicum*) by mistake. A natural hybrid, the Russian comfrey was no use for gum, but Doubleday, who was also a smallholder, thought the bountiful plant might have potential as a fodder crop. Britain was still dealing with the aftermath of the Irish potato famine and Doubleday hoped to develop a crop that could ameliorate the effects of famine. He set out to improve the variety by selecting the best plants with the highest yields. (Whether he succeeded would never be known: his working papers were destroyed after his death.)

Hills who had rented an acre of land at Bocking near Braintree in Essex now set up his own trials to investigate and categorise the different forms of British comfrey. He named the comfrey cultivars after the Bocking trial grounds.

In his *Organic Gardening* (1977) he invoked a banking metaphor to put his message across: 'Comfrey is so rich in protein...that it is a kind of instant compost. It has roots that go down 4 - 8 feet, which is deeper than most fruit trees, but instead of locking up the minerals in the wood where only fire and fungi can release them, it keeps them all in a "current account", as it were, ready for immediate use by crops.'

His leading variety for the kitchen garden was Bocking 14, 'a semi-sterile hybrid between *Symphytum asperum* from Russia and the wild *Symphytum officinale*, the herbalists' comfrey.' Hills founded an organisation to spread the word - and the comfrey - naming it after the Quaker, the Henry Doubleday Research Association (HDRA). A networking group that relied on feedback from its member gardeners, it grew quickly. By the start of the 1970s there were 17,000 members sharing their own ideas on organic gardening while Hills' wife Cherry shared her thoughts on vegetable nutrition: she raised early concerns, for example, of a possible link between aluminium cooking pans and Alzheimer's disease.

As the organisation grew two young scientists, Alan and Jackie Gear, responded to an advertisement in *The Times*: 'Young couple wanted to work on an organic research station. Full board. No pay' and joined HDRA. In the 1980s as Lawrence Hills handed the running of the organisation over to the Gears, the couple moved HDRA to its new home, then a run-down, wind-swept 22-acre smallholding near Coventry at Ryton-on-Dunsmore.

Fifty Tales from the Kitchen Garden

Hills died in the 1990s. By then HDRA had attracted a membership of around 30,000 and become the largest organic horticultural organisation in Europe with the future king of England, the Prince of Wales, as its patron. Ryton was now home to sample organic gardens devoted to ornamental vegetables, different methods of growing vegetables and a children's vegetable patch. There were other exhibition plots at Yalding in Kent and the vegetable garden at Audley End had been restored. HDRA, later rebadged as Garden Organic, had set up a heritage seed library to rescue old and odd vegetable varieties and were supporting farmers in developing countries to grow organic vegetables. 'Provided we do not drive our soils too hard, the land will go on feeding us through the sunlit centuries when motoring is but a memory,' Hills had predicted. HDRA had set out to show how it could be done.

Book II - Vegetable Husbandry

12. The Potting Shed

The potting shed, which according to the 1931 *New Gresham English Dictionary* was originally a sloping roof or penthouse to shed off the rain, was an essential item in the vegetable garden. The shed rose to prominence during the gardening boom of the mid-1800s. It became home to old seed catalogues and cropping plans, broken tools awaiting repair, discarded kitchen scales for weighing produce and a patched up chair or two. It was also a sanctuary in wet weather where the solitary gardener might peruse his or her gardening catalogue. (See *The Secret of Seed Sales*)

Unrestrained by editorial accuracy, they could be as quietly entertaining as this one from Sutton's in 1879: 'From Mr. E. Y. Yeatman Gardener to the Rev. E.C. Ince. "Your Royal Berks Marrow Pea has done remarkably well with me. It was included in the first prize collection of vegetables at the Watford Horticultural Show."' And from Mr William Morton of Shepton Mallet: 'With your Wordsley Wonder Pea I have had in many cases pods with 13 Peas in a pod, and (in one instance only) the, to me, unparalleled number of 14 in a pod'.

Garden catalogues not only promised dream crops, but also offered architectural and garden ornaments that were guaranteed to lure friends and admirers into the kitchen garden. There were fountains for the dipping pond, sundials, dove cots and beehives for the fenced garden, and follies, glasshouses and rustic summer houses. And there were sheds. The English villa gardener, for example, could spend a profitable Saturday afternoon reconstructing his Portable Hexagon Summer-House (£22) that 'can easily be put together by two persons in one hour'. If he so chose, he could specify one of the 'Tenant's Fixtures' marketed by manufacturer William Cooper on the Old Kent Road in London. 'This house is made in sections and can easily be put together or taken down and removed.' Ideal for the Victorian back-to-back, such modest structures would have been out of place in the spacious traditional walled gardens of the local *manoir* or country house. Here the sheds and outhouses might include a potting hut, garden office, seed store, tool room and root store along with a bate room (bate was the gardener's mid day meal) and the bothy (small hut) for the water boy. However the Victorian 'Tenant's Fixture,' delivered in sections by pony and trap and wrestled with for hours despite the easy construction promise, heralded the arrival of the flat-pack craft of shed making, or constructing its smarter sisters, the summer house, studio or garden office.

The home made shed reached its apotheosis on the allotment. Relatively free of building constraints and more reliant on recycled lumber and cast offs than store-bought materials, the allotment gardener gained a reputation for creativity and ingenuity when it came to making a shed. One listing structure was built from thrown-away glazed window frames; another from sea shore flotsam and jetsam; a third, with its port-holes and water barrel, was made to mimic a little tank locomotive.

Fifty Tales from the Kitchen Garden

Away from the allotment the garden shed might be transformed into desirable style statements of chic eco living spurred on by Shed of the Year competitions and artsy photo shoots. Most lone vegetable growers, however, resisted the lure of shed fame. In the 1990s Eric Kirten provided an informal tour of his shed on the site of Nottingham's oldest allotments, Hunger Hill. Hunger Hill had originally been bequeathed to the city by the monarch of the time so that the land rents could be spent on the upkeep of the bridge over the River Trent. The rents were reduced in 1606 following complaints over the cost of fencing the land against 'the deere lying in ytt'.

With the 'deere' long gone, Eric had lavished random care on his den, built with brick and recycled planks, old doors and abandoned windows. A small wood stove fuelled on skip lumber warmed the comfortable chaos of its interior where a potting bench was littered with seed catalogues, seedlings in yoghurt pots and spilled trays of potting compost. The walls were decorated with out-of-date nude calendars: 'It's a place of retreat,' he explained.

The retreat might be from an unhappy marriage, a trauma (many shell shocked survivors from the 20th century's two world wars found sanctuary in their garden sheds) or even a housing crisis. David Crouch and Colin Ward in *The Allotment* (1988) record how, in the home-hungry days of the early 1900s, many families were forced to live in the brick-built summerhouses on Hunger Hill. At least one woman was born there and raised a family of eight.

The shed or shack could even become a place of therapy. In Australia during the 1990s men's sheds projects sprang up at Tongala in Victoria and the Lane Cove Community Shed in New South Wales. Focussed on the mental health and well being of men, the men's sheds movement began its worldwide spread. It was a response to a growing problem in the western world: suicide. In 2014 three times more men than women had killed themselves in the United Kingdom; in Finland young men aged between 15 and 19 were killing themselves at the rate of one a week; and in the state of Wyoming, USA, 80 per cent of all suicides were men. Many people hoped that, by promoting better social interaction, the men's shed movement could help miserable men.

13. Hedge and Fence

Good fences make good neighbours. They also make good kitchen gardens and the need to fence the vegetable plot has exercised gardeners for centuries. Hedges, sunken fences, walls and wide water courses all played their part.

Water was an effective way to keep predators off the kitchen garden. It could keep them in too; in medieval times a water-filled ditch was often used to contain the rabbit warren and ensure a supply of fresh meat. A ready water supply also allowed for regular watering and a place to grow willows and rushes for turning into ties and baskets.

In pre-Roman Britain, at least, there was no need to fret about rabbit fencing since the coney had yet to be introduced, but there were other beasts to worry about from bears and beavers to wolves. Even as late as the 12th century, long after the Romans had withdrawn to Italy, the monks of Llanthony Priory on Wales' English borders were plagued by a surplus of wolves (and rebellious Welshmen). In 1135 they abandoned their monastery in the remote Black Mountains for the relative safety of Gloucester.

 Bill Laws

Once the wolves were gone, marauding deer and cattle might still devour the labourer's winter supplies of leeks and coleworts. While rapacious animals might pester the peasant, there were also light-fingered passers-by to be contended with. Where there was no shortage of rock, householders soon learned to protect their plot with a dry stone wall.

Some of the oldest stone walls in Europe were exposed when in 1850 a wild storm swept away the sand that had hidden the walls of Skara Brae, Orkney for 4,000 years. The silvered stone boundaries that crisscross Britain's limestone uplands were infants by comparison, built during the monastic wool trade of the 1200s and 1300s. The golden limestone walls of the Cotswolds gardens came still later: most date back to the 1700s and 1800s when the common lands of the people were appropriated by the wealthy landowners.

Ireland, like the Mediterranean countries, supported generations of skilled dry stone wallers and it was migrant Irish labourers, escaping the famine, who built the miles of Kentucky's famous rock fences. The waller's craft varied from region to region, the Cotswold's masons topping their walls with stones laid on their sides (combers), while in the Peak District of England they had a preference for upright coping stones laid in what was affectionately known as a hen and cock style. The Celts of Cornwall and west Wales, meanwhile, favoured earthen banks reinforced with a herringbone pattern of stone and topped with a thorn hedge.

And it was the thorn hedge that caught Emperor Caesar's eye as he pushed through northern Europe during the Gallic wars of 58–50BC. 'These hedges present a barrier like a wall,' wrote the Roman general in surprise. (His centurions were masters of the defensive barricade: emperor Hadrian's wall, begun around 170 years later to separate the savage Highland tribes of Scotland from the conquered southerners, is the largest monument of

Fifty Tales from the Kitchen Garden

Roman times.) The living hedges that Caesar encountered were also, and still are, protected by a ditch to keep browsing cattle at bay. They were made then, as now, with saplings of thorn and oak, crab and hawthorn, holly and field maple protected by a temporary stake and pole fence. Within a decade the saplings would have grown tall enough to be laid, when the sap was down, during the winter. The hedger used his cutting hook to slice into the wood, near the base of the sapling and, bending it over the cut, wove it around fresh wood stakes taken from the surplus hedge timber. The top of the hedge would be finished with a whippy rail of willow or hazel taken from a small willow bed or coppiced hazel grove nearby, kept for the purpose of providing spare parts for the hedger.

As a living barrier the hedge yielded autumn fruits and dead wood for the kitchen fire: 'Euerie (every) hedge/hath plenty of fewell and fruit,' as Thomas Tusser pointed out in his *Five Hundred Pointes of Good Husbandrie*. Anyone caught stealing the 'fewell' faced being whipped until they 'bled well' for in medieval times the offence of hedge breaking was a serious matter. The hedge breaker might also be expected to compensate the landowner who had to call on the hedge mender to make good the damage. In the northern hemisphere the hedge mender was said to be the figure of the man on the moon, a dim-witted individual carrying a fork load of thorns on his back to repair a hedge.

A dead hedge was an acceptable, if not a particularly sustainable, alternative to the living hedge. Once again traditions varied from region to region. In Estonia, tall hazel rods, or ethers, were woven between three poles laid horizontally. In Sweden pine poles secured together with twists of bark were rested on timber supports at an angle of 45 degrees. In north and west Wales fangs of slate, stone waste taken from the quarries, were

 Bill Laws

stood on end and wired together in imitation of the picket or paling fence.

The picket, or pale, originated from the Roman *palus*, a stake used both to reinforce the timber defences of their wall forts and laid, spike up (as a 'picket'), in ambush trenches in front of their walls. (Hadrian's Wall was protected in this way.) In the context of the kitchen garden, and in modern city suburbs from Adelaide to Phoenix, Arizona the dog-eared picket (dog-eared referring to the pointing of the picket) is a cherished domestic barrier designed to keep the kids in and the dogs out - or vice versa.

The primary purpose of the picket or pale in the Middle Ages was not to protect the kitchen garden, but to keep fallow deer in their proper place: the nobleman's park. Medieval pales were made from split or cleft oak stakes set in the ground and pinned to horizontal rails. A bank and ditch were added as an additional measure to keep the deer from straying, the pale fence being run along the top of the bank. Such a fence was not only employed to conserve his lordship's stock of venison: in Ireland, following the conquest of Henry II, the English settled within the area fenced off against the Irish, referred to as The Pale. Those living 'beyond the pale' were considered beyond redemption.

Once the gardener had enclosed the growing plot with picket, ditch, hedge, fence or wall, he or she soon became aware of an unexpected benefit: a walled garden is a warm garden.

14. The Walled Garden

The physical walled gardens of the 19th century were not so different from the digital walled gardens of the 21st, those closed software systems that presented the provider with absolute control over content and applications: both offered privacy, sanctuary and a modest amount of protection from the wicked world outside.

In an unusually contemplative mood Keith Ruck, the former head gardener of a 17th century manor on the Welsh borders, considered the merits of the brick walled garden at Pontrilas Court. 'There is something about working in the walled garden. The atmosphere is like working in a church.' He remembered the garden's glory days when in the 1960s, to raise funds for the community, the grounds were thrown open to the public. 'I always remember there'd be hundreds of people milling round. Then, at dusk when they'd gone home and you'd go down to shut some lights up or something, you'd turn in the doorway when you was coming out from there [the walled garden] and it almost feels like you got to shut the door quietly. I've heard other old gardeners say the same: you almost think like you got to show a bit of reverence.'

The preferred material for the walled garden was brick not least because a brick wall raised the temperature within the garden by a degree or two. People have been making and using bricks for 6,000 years. However, in their most durable form, hard baked in a fire so as to make them withstand the weather, it was the Romans, as usual, who took the technology across Europe. The Roman bricks, used mostly as a bonding course to hold stone or rubble masonry in place, were so broad and thin that they looked more like a tile (from *tegula* or *tegere*, to cover). Being less than two inches (5 centimetres) thick meant that they were well baked in the kiln. This durability has allowed Roman brickwork to survive in remarkably good condition to this day. It also explains why the use of brickwork continued to flourish across the continent long after the conquering Romans had been vanquished. (Except in Britain: the departure of the Romans marked a famine of brickwork in that country that lasted a thousand years.)

Being fire-resistant, cheap and attractive, brick was judged ideal for the walling although other materials used included cob, pisé (rammed earth), chalk, timber and even plate glass mounted on iron frames. Temporary timber walls were another alternative and one design involved timber walls made of deal planks against which were heaped middens of hot manure. They were so successful, according to one commentator, that the kitchen gardener could raise 'gooseberries fit for tarts' in January. American settlers regarded brickwork not only as a fine defence against fire, but as a sign of status, both in the house and garden.

In the late 1770s at Monticello in Virginia Thomas Jefferson constructed a ten foot (3.04 metre) timber paling fence around his vegetable 'patch' (the 10 acre - 4.04 hectares - plot contained 24 growing plots) to keep out predatory wildlife. However at the

Fifty Tales from the Kitchen Garden

University of Virginia, which he founded a dozen years after terracing his kitchen garden, he had employed brickwork to enclose the Pavilion Gardens. Rather than build them straight Jefferson adopted a serpentine design. Rounded, 'crinkle crankle' walls or *slangenmuren* (snake walls), had been popular in Britain during the late 1700s and early 1800s. They did not meet with the approval of Thomas Hitt, gardener to Lord Robert Manners at Bloxholme in Lincolnshire who dismissed serpentine walls in his *A Treatise of Fruit Trees* (1755) as 'attended with evils of one kind or other. Though walls built with curves have, in calm seasons the benefit of more heat than others; yet, in windy weather, the winds...rebounding from side to side, break and destroy the tender branches and blossoms of trees.'

Within the walled garden, the conventional square- or rectangular-shaped garden was traditionally quartered by four vegetable plots surrounded by paths and wall-side borders. Their dimensions reflected the size of the household: at Holkham in Norfolk, for example, the walls enclosed no less than six acres. Walled gardens were orientated slightly to the west of south so that the heat of the early afternoon was concentrated on one wall. This sun-trap wall, which stored the heat and released it through the chill night, was usually built higher than the other walls so as to make the most of its position. It was a fine site for fruit: figs, vines, peaches, apricots and nectarines would be planted against the south west walls and late fruiting plums, gooseberries, currants and morello cherries against the north wall.

One garden writer advocated covering the walls in metal to reflect the heat into the garden although there is no evidence that his suggestion was put into practise. The garden designer Humphry Repton liked to build walled gardens with six or seven sides while the gardening author, William Robinson, built his walled garden at Gravetye, Sussex in an oval shape. He used dressed stone rather than brick because, he believed, the stone's smooth surface afforded fewer hiding places for insects.

Fires might be lit inside the walled garden to counter frosts; they were even lit beneath the soil to force fruit, but a more effective way to raise the temperature or limit frost damage was to heat the walls themselves. Hot or flued walls were used in kitchen gardens from the mid 1700s, the tell-tale signs for garden historians being the small cast-iron doors or framed stones set in the wall to clean out the flues. Flues in some walls, however, were simply made large enough for the chimney sweep's children to climb in and clean. (At Fonthill in Wiltshire, the work was carried out, allegedly, by the estate's Jamaican dwarves.) Heated walls were eventually superseded by heated glasshouses built against the walls.

In Britain the introduction of a tax on bricks in 1750 had slowed the pace of walled garden construction, but by 1850, when the tax was repealed, the demands of country house guests on the produce of the vegetable garden made the walled kitchen garden as necessary as a polite parlour maid or a deferential butler. By the time of Queen Victoria's coronation in 1837, the walled kitchen garden was a fashionable favourite, but a century later, without the workforce required to tend them, they were crumbling into disrepair. Even as the walled garden spiralled into a near terminal decline, organisations such Britain's Walled Kitchen Gardens Network were formed to save, preserve and help owners restore what remained. Reminding gardeners of the need to hand on this 'rich asset to future generations', the Network spoke hopefully of a coming renaissance of walled kitchen gardens.

15. Blanching

Who knows when the first person noted the effects of blanching their crops? The term started to appear in the late 1700s, the name harking back to the long suffering Blanche of Castille (1188–1252), the queen of France who bore at least twelve children. While in that nation the name Blanche remained popular it fell from favour in America after the arrival of the tempestuous Blanche Du Bois in Tennessee Williams' *Street Car Named Desire*.

The French word, meaning white or pale, was applied to the process of preventing photosynthesis in order to produce a sweet, white and tender leaf. Blanching was carried out by gardeners assiduously binding their lettuce leaves together, burying their endive in trenches or heaping soil or sand around the beet leaves.

Chicory and celery might be buried fresh in barrels of sand (upside down to keep the sand out) until they blanched. Or else they might be enveloped in earth and covered with a warming layer of horse dung. Seakale, which could be blanched in the garden under a clay pot like rhubarb, was also naturally blanched where it grew on the sea shore, by piling beach stones and pebbles around the stems.

16. Muck and magic

How do you grow good vegetables? The answer, as one British radio comedian Kenneth Williams used to say, lies in the soil. That soil had to be constantly improved and the traditional improver was manure. 'Be avaricious for manure, and always keep your mind in firm conviction that your ground is in an impoverished state,' advised Shirley Hibberd. But what constituted 'manure'? A comprehensive list from the early 1800s included sea weed, spoiled hay, tanner's spent bark, Cornish pilchards and Fenland sticklebacks, whale blubber ('good reports from Surrey'), horn and bone, hair, woollen rags, blood, coral, urine, pigeon dung and the dung of domestic fowls, cattle, oxen, sheep, deer and camels, street and road dung, soot, soapers' waste and 'house sweepings'. A Mr Young reported an experiment where a field was spread with herrings and ploughed in for wheat. The crop, however, was 'so rank' it was 'laid before harvest.'

The use of street sweepings continued into the 1920s and 1930s as gardener Keith Ruck recalled. 'In those days around Abergavenny [in Wales] they had the linesman, as they was called, and they used to cut the sides of the road. Put a line down and

Fifty Tales from the Kitchen Garden

no twists and all done perfect there. The leaves were all swept up and then all that was put in tumps along the side of the road. Some of the farmers had horse and carts under contract to the council for collecting it up. We used to get them to tip it near the bottom of the garden. Then, when that was rotted, we used to sieve it all out and use it for a seed compost.'

For his liquid manure feed Keith's father would take an old tar barrel, burn out the remaining tar and fill it with pond water. 'We used to scrounge round all the farms for when the farmers were *dagging*, that was cleaning the rear ends of lambs and sheep before shearing. We used to collect all those, put 'em in a hessian sack and hang them in the barrel. That was our liquid feed. You couldn't beat it.'

For solid manuring, the vegetable garden was double dug or trenched, a method involved digging a trench two spits of a spade deep, laying the bottom of the trench with well rotted manure and covering it with soil excavated from the next row along. Some writers, possibly those who could pay the gardener to do it for them, advocated a back-breaking trench three spits deep. Professional gardeners knew the two-spit deep method as bastard trenching (the explanation that it was a bastard of a job is unfounded) and a bed might be bastard trenched every four or five years.

Another way to keep the ground in good heart was to leave the plot 'fallow' for a year. The term fallow, as in fallow deer, referred to the pale red or pale yellow colour of land that has been turned, or ploughed, but left unsown.

Apart from perennials such as Jerusalem artichokes or asparagus, most vegetables were planted in spring. Half of the crops - onions, peas, beans and salads - was harvested within six months, and the remainder over the rest of the year. A rule of thumb to avoid the ground getting tired was never to

 Bill Laws

follow a crop with another of the same family. 'A studied rotation is advisable. The kitchen garden should be divided into a number of portions, and a journal or notebook should be kept, with a reference to their numbers,' advised one head gardener, Mr Nicol, in his *Kitchen Gardener* of 1802.

Through the 1900s the more intensive four crop rotation saw potatoes, legumes, brassicas and roots trooping after one another around the plots. Heavy manuring and deep digging for the potato crop benefited the beans and peas that followed. Their nitrogen fixing roots aided the growth of the brassicas while the final root crop would grow straight and true. In his *Organic Gardening* (1977) Lawrence D Hills advocated a four crop rotation with four beds to fit into a standard allotment or 'two beds, one on each side of the centre path of the average 1930s-built semi-detached house garden.' His practical description evokes the suburban back garden with its 'cropping space, bush fruit, herb bed near the kitchen door, tool shed and compost bin behind the garage, and the lawn crossed by the clothes line.'

While every good gardener knew how to fertilise the soil, they were hard pressed to explain the process. During the 1200s researchers at the University of Bologna conducted careful experiments with seeds and plants (they had hoped to turn base metals into gold), yet the secret of soil fertility eluded them. Cardinal Nicholas of Cusa (1401–1464), a German astronomer who weighed soil and plant before and after the crop matured, discovered that the soil's weight had altered little. Water, he concluded, played a significant part in the process. By the mid 1800s another German Justus von Liebig (1803–1873), the founder of organic chemistry, showed that plants took in carbonic acid, water, ammonia, potassium, calcium, magnesium, phosphate and sulphate, converting them into starch, sugar, fat and proteins. Further more, he confirmed that animals, which ate and excreted plants, returned these elements to the soil. He was nearly, but not quite there, and it fell to the German botanist Julius von Sachs (1832–1897) to identify the essential minerals. He omitted the actual soil from his list and in 1860 he astonished the horticultural world by growing soilless plants hydroponically in mineral-fed water.

As the pace of horticultural research quickened John Bennet Lawes (1814–1900) and Joseph Gilbert (1817–1901) working at Lawes' family home, Rothamsted Manor in Hertfordshire, devised the ingredients for an artificial manure. Within half a century gardeners were producing remarkable results with their new 'fertiliser' chemicals: nitrate of soda, nitrate of potash or sulphate of ammonia, sulphate of potash, superphosphate of lime. Potash developed the sugars and starches in potatoes and tomatoes especially while nitrogen inputs were fast working and produced vigorous green plants. But there was a spectre on the horizon: chemical contamination.

When scientists revealed that the once useful pesticide Dichloro-diphenyl-trichloroethane or DDT had entered the global food chain, vegetable gardeners began to wonder what they were doing to their soils – and to themselves. The garden world was becoming a potentially poisonous place with residuals such as antibiotics, copper, pesticides, herbicides, cadmium and lead lurking in modern manures and composts. The indications were that the high productivity produced by fearsome pesticides and chemical fertilisers in the kitchen garden could prove to be environmentally damaging. Many turned to the organic lobby and the prophet of the new organic age Lawrence Hills.

In the 1970s with high inflation and the cost of food rising Hills predicted that many would be forced to try for self sufficiency 'as peasants do in many countries. With skilled gardening and

a rotation that crops through the winter, the 300 square yards of the standard allotment can produce nearly a ton and a half of food in a year,' he declared. There were plenty of people ready to try. Their first task was to master the mysteries of the compost heap.

17. The Compost Heap

While sailors and climbers have their knots, truck drivers and travelling salespeople their preferred routes from A to B, vegetable gardeners have their compost heaps. 'You have one source of the very best manure in the household, and you must treasure every scrap of stinking rubbish, solid and liquid, and not waste so much as a dead cabbage leaf,' trumpeted Shirley Hibberd. It was not a new idea. In the 1800s gardeners had collected highway manure, grass, weeds, mud from ditches, leaves, soot-ashes, and household refuse, mixing them together 'in the dunghill, and turned frequently over before using'.

A century later the war-time gardener writer Arthur J Simons was reminding his readers: 'The increasing shortage of stable manure, arising out of the decay of horse transport and the difficulty of obtaining any kind of animal manure in and around towns...have combined to encourage the conversion of vegetable waste of the garden into manure by the making of compost heaps.' He went on to describe no less than six different methods of making compost including the Indore process and the 'Quick Return'.

 Bill Laws

Confusion has arisen over the term compost being applied to fine sterile soil used as a medium for raising seeds, seedlings and plants (See John Innes' Revolutionary Potting Composts). Compost in the traditional sense was a mixture of vegetable matter, soil, water, air and in some instances an activator, which was allowed to decay. The resulting humus was applied to improve the garden soil.

The key to the fermentation of a compost heap was the presence of nitrogen, which acted as a starter and accelerated the digestion of material into humus. Dung, rich in phosphates, and urine, rich in nitrogen and potash, were powerful activators. The best dung, insisted the Muslim gardeners of Spain in the 1400s, came from the best animals: the manure of a corn-fed stallion was infinitely preferable to that of the tired pack horse grazed on poor hay. Top of the list was bird dung, not least because the dung and urine were so neatly packaged into one dropping. Journals from St Peter's in Gloucester record that the mountains of dove droppings from inside the dovecote or columbaria were shovelled out on to the garden twice a year. And there was no point in wasting good urine: in the 1300s Ibn Bassal advised that labourers be encouraged to urinate on the compost. The Roman Columella commended human urine especially if it was stored for six months and mixed with 'old oil lees' before being applied to the olive crop.

Lawrence Hills listed his top eight manure producers from horse, cow and pig to goat, chicken, rabbit and pigeon. 'Goat manure is perhaps the best general manure of the lot, because the goat is a browser rather than a grazer... but the finest activator manure of all is pigeon droppings.'

Until the unveiling of the latest design for the water closet at London's Great Exhibition of 1851, the vegetable soil was regularly 'sweetened' by the products of the privy. King Henry

Fifty Tales from the Kitchen Garden

III ordered 'a privy chamber to the Queen's garderobe' in 1296. The garderobe, the French word for a small chamber for storing clothes became, in the Middle Ages, the polite term for what was later called euphemistically the smallest room.

In 1941 Arthur J Simons was recommending the addition of night soil to the compost list. 'Night' soil (soil was from the French *souiller*, to sully or defile) referred to the practise of emptying the earth closet at night: 'About once a year a Negro we called Mister Elsey would come with his wagon and clean the vault of our privy,' recalled an American Carl Sandburg in John Pudney's *The Smallest Room*. 'His work was always done at night. He came and went like a shadow in the moon.' In England in the Middle Ages it was the work of the gong fermors (gong meaning a privy and fermors from the verb fey to cleanse).

Through the 1600s, 1700s and 1800s, there was a running battle over how long such manure should be allowed to 'ferment' before it was dug into the kitchen garden. In the 1800s 'desiccated night-soil' was sold in France as *poudrette*. In London, it was mixed with quick lime and sold in cakes under the name Clarke's desiccated compost. The Chinese too were said to 'have more practical knowledge of the use of manures than any other people existing,' according to one commentator who described how the peasants mixed their night soil with earth and fashioned them into saleable cakes.

Various attempts were made to mechanise the process of making manure safe for the vegetable plot. In 1860, Moule's Earth-Closet Company patented the Rev. Henry Moule's device for automatically discharging a quantity of dry earth into the latrine when pressure was exerted on the lavatory seat. Sales were slow because the contraption required a plentiful supply of dry, finely sifted earth: ensuring a supply meant purchasing a special earth drying and sifting stove for the purpose.

 Bill Laws

The Rev. Moule would like others of his class, expect the morning maid to empty the chamber pots daily on to the garden compost heap. The compost heap was, and still is, the ideal way to return to the soil as much organic matter as possible. The decomposing vegetation was home to millions of soil organisms that fed the soil, improved drainage on heavy soils and helped retain water on light soils. With or without *poudrette* it was judged to be a horticultural wonder

18. John Innes' Revolutionary Potting Composts

John Innes is to the garden what the Hoover is to the home thanks to the seed potting compost that bears his name. Born in 1829, Innes became a successful London property developer and land dealer. When he died in 1904 he left £325,000 to set up a horticultural research centre. The John Innes Horticultural Institute opened in Surrey, and was moved later to Norwich in Norfolk. Contrary to popular belief, the Institute never produced a gram of commercial potting composts - but it did invent the first successful formula.

It had been common for gardeners to rely on their own recipes for soils in which to grow seeds, slips and cuttings. A Mr Cushing who worked at a nursery in Hammersmith, London in 1812, divulged his own formula to the readers of the *Exotic Garden*: 'Loam, peat, and sand, seem to be the three simples of nature, if I may so call them, most requisite for our purpose; to which we occasionally add as mollifiers, vegetable or leaf mould, and well rotted dung; for the judicious mixture and preparation of which, composts may be made to suit plants introduced from any quarter of the globe.' Sometimes these composts were sterilised, but more often they were not and some soil-borne disease would summarily destroy the gardener's stock. Too much fertiliser added to the compost caused the plants to grow leggy and soft or weak; too little and they grew hard or slow growing. The John Innes composts, based on a mix of seven parts of soil or loam, three parts of peat and two of grit, were devised in the 1930s. They were the work of two researchers at the Institute, William Lawrence and John Newell. Lawrence and Newell had been frustrated in their efforts to grow standard Chinese primroses (*Primula sinensis*) for research purposes by variable composts. In the end they devoted six years to perfecting two standard composts, one for seed sowing and one for potting.

The John Innes Number 1, for sowing seed, rooting soft cuttings and pricking out or potting up young seedlings or rooted cuttings, carried only a small amount of nutrients. Number 2, for the general potting of vegetable plants and house plants into medium sized pots or boxes, contained double the amount of fertiliser. The nutrients, nitrogen for top growth, phosphates for root growth, potash for flowering and fruiting, and trace elements for colour and flavour, were perfectly balanced. The basic ingredient, loam, was made from rotted-down, stacked turf, which was sterilised before being added to sphagnum moss peat and coarse sand or grit to provide the right amount of drainage.

Later John Innes No 3 was introduced with a richer mixture for final re-potting of heavier feeding vegetables such as cucumbers and tomatoes, and mature plants and shrubs in interior planters or outdoor containers.

The composts became an industry standard and revolutionised the growing of seeds and plants in pots. Fifty years later, although the nutrients had changed, the basic formula remained the same.

19. The Findhorn Secret: Growth and Sensibility

To be 'a vegetable' is to lack sensibility. Aristotle accepted that vegetables had no sensations, but, he insisted, they did possess souls. In the 1900s a Viennese biologist, Raol Francé, declared that not only did vegetables and other plants move about freely, although on a time scale too slow for us to follow, they were also highly sensitive to either abuse or gratitude. Authors such as Peter Tompkins and Christopher Bird, in their *The Secret Life of Plants* celebrated the sensibility of sunflowers that turned, like incautious sun bathers, to face the sun as it travelled from east to west (hence their French name *tour de sol* and Italian *girasol*). 'Plants may ... be the bridesmaids at a marriage of physics and metaphysics,' suggested the authors. Three extraordinary vegetable growers were about to reveal that plants had allies in the spirit world.

They were an ex-Royal Air Force squadron leader, Peter Caddy, his wife Eileen and their friend Dorothy MacLean. The three had been running the Cluny Hotel in Scotland during the

1950s when they embarked upon a major life change. Moving to a scruffy caravan site in a remote part of north Scotland, which looked out across Findhorn Bay, they were determined to turn away from the materialist world and pursue a life of 'limitless love and truth'. Central to their aspirations was the raising and growing of vegetables.

There are diminishing returns to be had from most vegetables the further north you travel. Shorter growing seasons and fewer growing days, earlier and later frosts, and poor or indifferent soils all play a part. Peter Caddy found the soil at Findhorn as 'fine, dusty sand and gravel in which nothing grew but rough pointed grass'. Nevertheless he double dug the plot, laying the up-turned turves at the bottom of the trench and erecting a wind proof fence, recycled from a dismantled garage. The land was manured with seaweed and the produce of the compost heap.

The women, meanwhile sought spiritual guidance. Eileen, who had renamed herself Elixir, spoke of her midnight meditations and her vision of the run-down caravan park transformed into a place with seven cedar wood bungalows. Dorothy became Divina.

In their first year Divina, Elixir and the more prosaic Peter harvested onions, leeks, garlic, carrot, parsnip, swede, turnip, artichoke, kohlrabi, celery, marrow, potatoes, over twenty different kinds of salad and various herbs. In the autumn they pickled 14.8 pounds (6.75 kilograms) of red cabbage, bottles of cucumbers and put potatoes, carrots, beetroot, shallot, onion and garlic in store for the winter. In 1964 Peter Caddy grew a cabbage that weighed 44.6 pounds (20.25 kilograms). A single sprouting broccoli fed the group for weeks and was said to be too heavy to lift.

When Sir George Trevelyan, a leading member of the Soil Association and doyen of the New Age, visited the site, he was amazed at the fertility, growth and taste of the vegetables. Peter

Caddy revealed the Findhorn secret: Divina had made spiritual contact with whole hierarchies of plant spirits, or devas, who instructed her on how to make the most of the vegetables. She expounded on the theory that you are what you eat, explaining that plants fed the soul as well as the body: vegetables grown by a bad tempered gardener, for example, could themselves cause ill humour in those who ate them.

'You are perfectly free to say this is nonsense,' Trevelyan would later say in an interview. 'Here you are in the middle of the twentieth century and we're talking of fairies in your garden. But how else do you explain the plants that grow on these decayed sand dunes?'

Within 10 years Elixir's premonitions were fulfilled. Findhorn went on to become an established community of 300 people, wealthy enough to buy up the caravan park and replace the caravans with the seven cedar wood bungalows predicted by Elixir. Even the old Cluny Hill Hotel, as well as neighbouring properties, was purchased to house the expanding educational charity of Findhorn. The Findhorn vegetables had proved to be a strange success.

20. Rudolph Steiner's Biodynamic Vegetables

In 1982 the retiring Director of Agriculture for Tanganika wrote a book called *Bio-Dynamic Gardening*. John Soper had been a dutiful servant of the British colonial service. He had spent 32 years in East Africa and Malaya. Captured by the Japanese during World War Two he was made a prisoner of war for three and a half years. In his retirement he was to promote some unorthodox ideas on vegetable husbandry.

'More and more people today,' he wrote, 'are convinced in their heart that the world which we see and hear around us is not the only one; behind it and beyond the range of our senses there must be other worlds which underlie, inform, permeate and organise all our national surroundings.'

When Soper retired to work his vegetable and fruit patch, first in Hampshire and later at Clent, near Birmingham, he became a leading member of the Bio-Dynamic Association, a movement founded on the teachings of Rudolph Steiner.

Steiner, the son of an Austrian stationmaster, was born in 1861 and died in 1925. By the age of eight he had already experienced 'the reality of the spiritual world'. In his forties he was devoting himself to the 'science of the spirit,' or what he called anthroposophy. His writings and teachings help to found the Camphill villages, devoted to the care of people with learning disabilities, and Waldorf schools as well as methods of bio-dynamic farming and gardening.

In the 1920s Steiner's supporters were as concerned about agricultural trends as consumers were in the 1980s and when he presented a series of lectures on farming in 1924, his ideas on agriculture were adapted to form the basis of bio-dynamic vegetable gardening. Even ardent followers like Soper, however, found Steiner's notions difficult to follow: 'He emphasised that he was speaking from his personal experience on small peasant farms, and he did not mention gardens at all,' wrote Soper later. Nevertheless the bio-dynamic movement, based at the Goetheanum (the centre was designed by Steiner) at Dornach, Switzerland, has become a global influence on vegetable growers.

'The earth breathes, it has a respiratory system, it has a pulse, it is sensitive and it has a skin,' explained Soper. Break the skin with a cutting or landslide and it will heal itself in time with a protective layer of vegetation. The earthly life form expanded and contracted like any breathing being, said Soper and he suggested that the gardener work in harmony with the rhythms of this living sphere. For example, harvesting leaf vegetables and transplanting seedlings was best done in the expanding mornings while sowing seeds, harvesting root crops and transplanting small plants should be carried out during the evenings as the earth gently contracted.

 Bill Laws

Equally important to the growth of vegetables was the influence of the planetary rhythms. The parts of the plant - root, leaf, flower and fruit - mirrored the four elements - earth, water, air and light and fire - and all came under the influence of the moon, sun and the zodiac, that ring of twelve constellations against which the sun appears to move in the course of a year. Esoteric perhaps, but Soper pointed out how vegetables in the northern hemisphere grew to their climax as the sun drove on towards its summer solstice and then waned and ripened as it headed towards the autumn equinox. The moon, he argued was a mighty influence.

'Most authorities agreed that seed should be sown with a waxing moon,' insisted one writer in the 1800s. Native Americans sensibly looked for the star cluster Pleiades, or the Seven Sisters, to disappear from the spring sky before planting their seed since this signalled the beginning of frost-free nights. The Roman Paraclesus wrote of the moon's influence on plants and two thousand years later one Cornish head gardener, R. J. Harris, attributed his success at vegetable growing to following the four quarters of the moon. He was echoing the advice of John Worlidge who, in 1669, advocated regulating the performance of horticultural operations by the age of the moon. Worlidge declared that turnips or onions, sown when the moon was full, would not 'bulb out,' but send up flower stalks instead. A weak tree, he added, should be pruned as the moon waxed and a strong one as it waned.

The recipe book of the Elizabethan Elinor Fettiplace, *Ellinor Fettiplace's Receipt Book: Elizabethan Country House Cooking*, compiled in 1604 and published by her descendent Hilary Spurling in 1986, contained detailed advice on moon planting: 'Sow red Cabage seed after Allhallowentide [1 November], twoe dayes after the moone is at the full, & in March tiake up the plants & set from fowre foot each from other, you shall have faire Cabages for the Sumer; then sow some Cabage seeds a day after the full moone in Marche, then remove your plants about Midsomer, & they wilbee good for winter.'

In 1693 the French author of *The Complete Gardener*, Jean-Baptiste de La Quintinye dismissed the theory. 'I solemnly declare that after a diligent observation of the moon's changes for thirty years together, and an enquiry whether they had any influence in gardening, the affirmative of which has been so long established among us, I perceived that it was no weightier than old wives' tales, and that it had been advanced by unexperienced gardeners. Sow what sorts of grains you please, and plant as you please, in any quarter of the moon, I'll answer for your success, the first and last day of the moon being equally favourable.'

In the early 1800s Loudon, too dismissed the lunar influence as 'superstitious observances attendant on a rude state of society'. But John Soper held to his view that plants, which bore their crops above ground, would grow better when sown during a waxing moon while root crops would thrive when sown as the moon waned.

The bio-dynamic gardeners had first to familiarise themselves with their soil, taking a fist-full of moist earth and squeezing it into a lump. A sandy soil would fall apart, a clay soil form into a lumpy ball. A second test involved mixing a soil sample with water in a glass jar, shaking it up and allowing it to settle. Sand would fall to the bottom while clay formed a sludge-like mix at the top.

Having established the nature of their soil, the bio-dynamic gardener could cultivate it with respect because, on planet earth, every gardener and every garden was an individual. Deep digging and trenching was reserved for heavy clay soils while light, sandy soils required little cultivation and benefited from

being sheltered from the elements with a cover crop of weeds when it lay fallow.

Horticultural pesticides and artificial fertilisers were to be avoided: 'One fact does appear to be fairly certain,' wrote Soper. 'The effects are partially or wholly negatived by the use of artificial fertilisers and agricultural poisons which deaden the soil's sensitivity and responsiveness.' Instead the bio-dynamic gardener should 'enliven' the soil with special composts or manures. Their preparation was positively sacramental. Preparation 500, for example, involved stirring 1.58 ounces (45 grams) of 'horn manure,' made from cow dung, for an hour in about three gallons of lukewarm water. The container had to be free from all forms of contamination, the water was best taken from a spring, the stirring stick had to be chosen to 'suit personal convenience' and the stirring method was specific. 'Stir briskly until a deep crater is formed in the rotating liquid; then quickly reverse the direction of stirring and continue until the deep crater is formed once more.' The aim was to create a whirling liquid 'in a seething, chaotic turbulence' and the concoction had to be used within the hour, either sprayed on to the garden or flicked out of a bucket with a bunch of twigs. Soper's explanation for the benefits of this enlivening mixture proved a step too far for some vegetable growers. 'Their main purpose is to stimulate and enhance the supersensible forces and influences working in from the far spaces of the cosmos and up from the centre of the earth.'

But the basics of biodynamics - helping to heal the earth, especially in the kitchen garden - proved to have a universal appeal. Now involved in related issues such as animal welfare, genetically modified food and sustainable farming, the international movement founded on Steiner's theories and Soper's interpretations shows no sign of running out of new recruits.

21. Britain's Kitchen Gardens

A century ago the idea of opening the kitchen garden to interested visitors would have seemed as odd as offering public tours of the coal cellar. The flower garden and shrubbery were the proper place for decorative delights, not the functional workplace that was kitchen garden.

Yet now gardens open to the public are inclined to include a kitchen garden in the tour; some like Heligan and Audley End have founded their reputations on their vegetable borders. Clearly people are genuinely interested in the plantings, the patterns and the structures of the vegetable plot.

While there is no economic imperative for people to grow their own fruit and vegetables (as there is during any down turn in the economy), waiting lists for allotments continue to grow in proportion to the scale of protests (even from non-gardeners) whenever plans are unveiled to redevelop them.

Garden fashion has played its part in stimulating this vegetal interest, from the Arts and Crafts garden, where a trellis work of runner beans forms part of the romance, to William Robinson's and Gertrude Jekyll's popularising of the cottage garden with its intimate mix of flowers, fruit and vegetables. Then there are the increasing number of cross over vegetables such as ruby chard, orach or a plain pattern of lettuce, which add a dash of interest to the informal flower border. But perhaps the interest in the fruits of the vegetable plot comes from the fact that people like to grow what they eat, and eat what they grow.

Bayleaf gives a glimpse into how a medieval kitchen garden might have looked. Bayleaf is a rescued Wealden hall house set in the grounds of the Weald and Downland Open Air Museum in West Sussex. The garden, recreated in front of the house, was designed with six plots of vegetables worked in a three-year rotation. Leeks, leaf beet and parsley are planted in the first year, coleworts or collards in the second, while in the third year the plots are manured during the winter then planted with onions the following spring. In summer all the plots come alive with colour as the undercrop of edible weeds, which are allowed to self seed each year, come into flower.

The oldest parts of Bayleaf date to back to the 1400s. Four centuries later Queen Victoria made a handsome £50,000 from the sale of the old kitchen gardens at Kensington Palace, London. The money did not linger long in the royal coffers. The Queen and her husband Albert ploughed it back into a new kitchen garden at Windsor. Founded on the same principles as any other manor house kitchen garden of the time, it was built with a walled garden, hot houses and tool sheds. The scale of the enterprise, however, set it apart from the common lot.

One hundred and fifty gardeners worked within the 11.8 feet (3.6 metre) high outer and inner walls that encircled the 27 acre garden - it was eventually expanded to 50 acres. In place of conventional gates, a porter's gatehouse led into the gardens. The head gardener lived on site in a house with a special suite of rooms where Albert and Victoria could enjoy a cream

Fifty Tales from the Kitchen Garden

tea with fresh - very fresh - strawberries when they visited. There was an under gardener's house too, built close to over 787 feet (240 metres) of hot houses. There were boiler rooms, potting sheds, mushroom houses, forcing pots, stables and, as a centrepiece for the garden, a fountain set in a 29.5 feet (9 metre) diameter basin.

The post war fate that befell so many kitchen gardens would dispatch Victoria and Albert's kitchen garden too, leaving only its great walls behind. However, a century later another member of the royal family was planning a kitchen garden at his country house, Highgrove in Gloucestershire.

Prince Charles, the Prince of Wales, took advice from one of his neighbours, the garden author and lecturer Rosemary Verey. Her Cotswold manor home garden at Barnsley House was a model of the 20th century English arts and crafts style with its mixed borders, formal *potager*, classical temple and modern knot. She had also established a decorative vegetable garden based on the designs of William Lawson's *Country Housewife's Garden* of the 1600s (and prompted a revival in the popularity of ruby chard). A new kitchen garden was constructed at Highgrove similarly laid out as a decorative *potager*. Appropriately enough, given the spirit of the new age, the vegetable garden was to be run on organic lines.

The humble gardeners who managed these plots for their wealthy employers are rarely remembered, but William Cresswell made his mark: 'Received from Mr Bryan £3.9s.4d for month's wages, also notice to leave at end of next month,' he wrote in 1874. He was under gardener at Audley End near Saffron Walden in Essex and his diary, which petered out when he left Audley End, gave an insight into the life of the Victorian under gardener. William Cresswell had already contemplated leaving: 'Mr Bryan angry for not sending for him. Self troubled in mind with several

things lately taken place in affair connected with situation, had thought of giving notice to leave.'

Twenty-two-years-old when he arrived from Cambridge to work at Audley End, William Cresswell lived in the bothy next to the great glasshouses (one of the oldest and largest in the UK), enjoying the benefits of central heating from the hot water pipes that ran through the bothy and into the greenhouses. Attached to the stately Jacobean manor house of Audley End the walled vegetable garden, with over two miles of box hedging around the plots, fell into disuse in the Second World War when house and grounds were passed into the hands of the state. Later restored by the Henry Doubleday Research Association and English Heritage, the gardens were opened to the public and productive once again.

There are two Hampton Courts in England. The first, and more famous, is the Royal Palace near London, its gardens opened to the public by Queen Victoria in 1838. The second, in the rural West Midlands, features an imaginative decorative kitchen garden. It opened its gardens to the public in the 1990s.

Hampton Court was founded in the early 1400s after the owner, Sir Roland Leinthall, 'toke many prisoners' at the battle of Agincourt, 'by which prey he beganne the new buildings of Hampton Court,' according to one commentator. The manor followed the fortunes of many a rich man's house, one moment in favour and the subject of vast expenditure, at another in the doldrums, languishing in decay. The estate was purchased and sold by a succession of owners including knights, a viscountess, a Member of Parliament and a petro-chemical multi national, before being rescued by a wealthy American couple.

In 1810 the estate, which had changed hands only once in the previous four centuries, was bought by Richard Arkwright, said to be the wealthiest commoner in England after his father

Fifty Tales from the Kitchen Garden

made a fortune in the cotton industry. The upkeep of the estate was to drain the resources of three generations of the family over the next century. In the 1840s Joseph Paxton, the architect of the Crystal Palace, designed a new conservatory for the Court. At the close of the century owner Johnny Arkwright patented a successful design for a wooden box made to carry vegetables and fruit without damaging the contents. It was not enough to restore the wealth of the Arkwrights who sold up in 1911. The house changed hands six more times before Americans Robert and Judith Van Kampens bid unsuccessfully for the estate at auction. Nevertheless they visited the house out of curiosity in 1994, met the vendors and within ten minutes had agreed a sale.

The Van Kampens were reputed to have spent $17.5 million on the restoration of the house and gardens. The Van Kampen gardens, designed by artist and gardener Simon Dorrell, have been described as one of the most ambitious garden creations of the 1990s. The design included a maze of a thousand yews with a gothic tower at its centre. Below the tower an underground tunnel led to a waterfall and a sunken garden. But key to the design were the flowers and decorative vegetables laid out within the original Victorian garden walls and divided up by canals, a pair of octagonal pavilions and pleached avenues of lime trees. Organic produce from the kitchen garden was used to supply a restaurant housed in Paxton's restored glasshouse. Hampton Court and its extraordinary vegetable garden was sold when Robert Van Kampen died in 1999.

Clumber Park near Worksop in Nottinghamshire was another aristocratic rural retreat. In 1772 the kitchen garden supplied fresh vegetables and fruit to the 100 strong household of the Dukes of Newcastle. Garden walls enclosed around four acres of land, but there was another six acres of ground under fruit and vegetable cultivation. It included an acre of glass housing,

 Bill Laws

forcing sheds and mushroom houses. Close by a pair of ice houses (See The Ice House) were used to store fresh produce. Even in the early 1900s the gardens required 29 full time gardeners to grow and harvest crops from everyday carrots and potatoes to exotics such as chillies, sweet corn, pineapple and sugar cane. In 1938 the manor house was destroyed, but the vegetable gardens and its 449 feet (137 metre) long glass house were saved and restored by the National Trust.

What was to become one of the most famous vegetable gardens of the 20th century started life as a kitchen garden in the late 1700s. Henry Hawkins Tremayne had been curate of Loswithiel in Cornwall when he unexpectedly inherited an estate. It was called The Willows, but went by the Cornish name for willow, Heligan. The family estate, which stretched from Gorran to Mevagissey was spread across a 100 acres of south west Cornwall. It was large enough to encompass several farms, its own flour mill, brick works, saw mill, brewery and a kitchen garden of nearly two acres. Produce from the garden not only helped to feed the family and their guests, but also the 20 inside staff and up to 22 outside employees. Henry Tremayne busied himself with Heligan, laying out the gardens more or less as they appear today. Three further generations carried on the horticultural work until June 1914 when two shots from an assassin's pistol in far away Sarajevo sounded what was to be the opening salvo of the First World War. It's doubtful whether Heligan's water boy or flowerpot cleaner knew anything about the incident, but already the political repercussions were rippling across Europe. By August of that year they were lapping against the walls of the big house.

'Don't come here to sleep or slumber,' scribbled one of the gardeners with his pencil on the lavatory wall. Each of his mates added their own names and the date: August 1914. By the time of the hollow victory of Armistice Day in 1918, only three of the twelve staff who had gone to war returned and Heligan, like so many other grand houses, went into a post war decline.

That was until one winter's day in 1999 when entrepreneurs Tim Smit and John Nelson went exploring and stumbled upon what Smit would later describe as the horticultural equivalent of the Marie Celeste. 'John and I stumbled across a tiny room buried under fallen masonry in a heavy shrouded corner of the walled garden. Here we found those barely legible signatures in its faded, lime-washed walls'.

Ambitiously they decided to restore Heligan. Early efforts were concentrated on the glasshouse fruits and the famous pineapple pit, but it was the 1.8 acre vegetable garden which became what Tim Smit called the engine room of the house. Whole trees and brambles four metres high were cleared from the plot. After ploughing and laying the water pipes, the classic cruciform of paths was relaid and, under the shade of fruit hoops, the four quarters of the vegetable garden were restored.

The Heligan gardeners, fixing a benchmark of the mid 1800s, set out to recreate the Victorian vegetable garden, selecting plants on the basis of taste and flavour and growing them without either the supposed benefits of modern pesticides, herbicides or fertilisers or the conventional garden poisons of the Victorian age such as nicotine, arsenic and red lead. Eventually Heligan was supplying its own restaurant and, with a vegetable box scheme, the local neighbourhood with produce from the kitchen garden.

Book III - Origins and Losses

22. A Vegetable Timeline

People have grown vegetables for eight thousand years at least. One theory - and it remains only a theory - supposes that vegetable cultivation was precipitated by the world's first famine. At some point in the past the planet's human population grew too large to feed itself on hunting and gathering alone. The natural balance between communities and wilderness had been reached and passed: from here on the human race would have to grow its own food if it was to survive.

If we contrive to represent the last twelve millennia as twelve months of a calendar year, we would find the Natufian people, who lived in the Middle East to the west of the river Euphrates, already gathering their wild cereals in January of that fictitious year. At the other end of the timeline, around December 27, the United Kingdom would be mourning the death of a keen vegetable grower, Gertrude Jekyll. She died in 1932.

In our mid January or 10,000 Before the Christian or Common Era (BCE) the ice sheets that had locked down Europe and North America finally began to melt. In the March of our vegetable year the earliest recorded vegetables were growing around Palestine.

Bill Laws

The early civilisations had settled in the Middle East, building their palaces and pyramids, towns, ports and, of course, kitchen gardens close to the irrigating rivers of the Tigris, Euphrates and Nile.

By mid April, vegetables were being grown around the borders of modern Iran and Iraq. In Crete the kitchen garden was established by May, in China and Mexico by June, and the Indus Valley of eastern India by August, 2500 BCE in real time.

Agriculture and its sister, horticulture, had been carried across the Indus plane by the Indus Valley civilisation by mid-July (3500 BCE). We know more about the visible surface of the moon than we do of this mysterious culture. Archaeologists have uncovered some of its village factories, but scholars are still wrestling with its language and deliberating on whether it should be read from the left or the right. Research has established that by 1700 BCE (or early September) the civilisation had collapsed, perhaps because of political instability, a shift in the course of the great Indus river itself, some other natural disaster such as an earthquake, or a combination of all three.

By mid September (1500 BCE) the ancient Egyptians, planting flowers in their vegetable plots, were growing gardens for pleasure as well as purpose. A literary Greek garden 'full of fruits, also sweet figs and bounteous olives' appears in early October in Homer's *Odyssey*. Later that month, or around 300 BCE, according to paleobotanists, there were celery, beet, carrot, brassicas and asparagus being grown in the southern Mediterranean and peas, vetch, wheat and barley in northern Europe.

The Romans acquired their gardening crafts from the Greeks and by the end of October (100 BCE) the Latin vegetable garden was as highly productive as it was highly advanced. As the empire expanded through Europe the Romans introduced their own favourites including garlic, onion, leeks, lettuce, mustard,

Fifty Tales from the Kitchen Garden

parsnip, skirret, turnip and radish. The collapse of the Roman Empire apparently led to the collapse of the kitchen garden. This may be due more to a lack of documentary evidence than a paucity of vegetable growers, but we must wait until mid November and the rise of the monastic garden before finding most Europeans enjoying a decent plate of vegetables again. They were still not described as vegetables - in early medieval times a herb described any garden plant useful as a pesticide, a medicine or for the pot. Not until the third week in November (around the year 700 CE) does the word vegetable creep into common use.

Culinary historians are still looking at establishing the genetic continuity between modern and medieval vegetables, but we would recognise many of the edible plants grown in the kitchen garden twelve centuries ago. Skirrets, garlic, plain-leaved parsley and the medieval broad bean, which can be traced back to the horse bean Maris Bead, were all on the menu. The medieval garden burgeoned with self-seeding salad crops such as fat hen and dandelion, the latter still a common enough salad crop. 'My Swiss-born mother used to cover the young dandelions with a dish to blanch them and keep the dogs from peeing on them,' recalls one young woman from Malvern while a French woman from Cholet remembers: 'Grandmother harvested *pissenlit* and served them with a salad dressing. They made you piss.'

Yellow or red onions, sown as seed or planted as sets, were grown along with green onions, that is any small or bull-necked onion eaten fresh rather than lifted and stored. They came under an assortment of names including ascalonia, fissiles, scallion, chibol, clumping winter onions and holeke. Holeke was the ever-ready onion, *Allium cepa var. perutile*, occasionally confused with the Welsh onion which was not Welsh at all, but 'foreign' from the Old German word Welsch or foreign. The true ciboule or spring onion *Allium fistulosum*, was a later arrival to Europe from Asia in the 1700s, or mid December of our vegetable year.

By early December, the Renaissance kitchen garden in Europe was well advanced. Meanwhile the last of Spain's Moorish leaders, Boabdil, had surrendered the keys to the city of Granada to his Christian conquerors. He left with a tear on his cheek, by the pass known as Ultimo Suspiro del Moro, the Moor's Last Sigh after the legendary remark of his mother: 'You do well to weep like a woman for what you failed to defend like a man.' Boabdil left behind a rich horticultural inheritance, still to be seen in places such as Valencia where the *huertas verduras*, the irrigated lands, grow hectare upon hectare of vegetables under the gaze of derelict Moorish castles.

By mid December, when Drake claimed California for England, the two-way vegetable traffic between America and Europe had reached fever pitch. For the next ten days, until Christmas Eve, the kitchen gardens of both continents flourished. In 1850 - or shortly after our Christmas Day - the Irish bogland potato crop failed.

Post Christmas and, apart from a growing frenzy in the kitchen garden during two world wars, the home-grown produce of the kitchen garden steadily diminished under a tidal wave of convenience and processed food. After the arrival of the 98 cent Swanson's TV dinner in America in 1954 came Vesta chicken curry, the first convenience food sold to UK housewives in 1962. But by the very end of December or the late 1900s, north Europeans had rediscovered what Mediterranean Europe had known all along: the best tasting vegetables are the ones you grow yourself.

23. Out of the East

Today upwards of 70 different vegetables can be grown in the kitchen garden and, until the opening up of the Americas in the 16th century, most originated in the Middle East. The story of how they reached the vegetable plot is a long and sometimes confusing one. Take the globe artichoke and its linguistic sister, the Jerusalem artichoke. The globe artichoke, *Cynara scolymus*, looks like what it is - an edible thistle. It first came into the kitchen 4,000 years ago when it was cultivated in the Middle East, in the fertile crescent that lay between the Nile and the Indus.

To the Greeks it was *kardos* or *skolumos,* to the Romans *carduus* which is why the Italians still enjoy their *cariofi*. The English name originates with the Arabian name *al-kharshuf.* In the depiction of Priapus on a fresco at Pompeii (see Artists and their Kitchen Gardens) weighing his monumental member against a tray of fruit and vegetables, the globe artichoke is there, possibly a reference to the artichoke's ancient reputation as an aphrodisiac.

Yet the Jerusalem artichoke, *Helianthus tuberosus*, was related neither to Jerusalem nor the globe artichoke. A member of the sunflower family, the Jerusalem artichoke came from what was to be Europe's second richest source of vegetables, the Americas. The edible part of the *kaishcucpenauk,* as the Algonquin Indians who lived in Michigan, Southern Quebec and Eastern Ontario called it, is the tuber and it was Samuel de Champlain (1567–1635), the one-time governor of French Canada who founded Quebec and mapped the Great Lakes, who reported that the *kaishcucpenauk* tasted of artichoke. The confusion was compounded when the appellation Jerusalem was added, either as a corruption of the Italian for sunflower, *girasole,* or of Terneusen, the Dutch village between Antwerp and Ostend that despatched artichokes to England in the early 1600s. (It was reported to be growing in Hampshire by 1617 by one John Goodyer.)

Having been cultivated by Native Americans, the *kaishcucpenauk* was growing wild from Georgia to Canada by the time the first European settlers arrived. The Pilgrim Fathers, however, viewed the Jerusalem artichoke with as much suspicion as the contemporary allotment holders who refer to it as the 'fartichoke,' in deference to its flatulent reputation. John Gerard had no time for the plant: 'In my judgement, which way soever they be drest or eaten, they are meat more fit for swine, than men.' In fact the Jerusalem artichoke or sunchoke, is very nutritious and valued as a sweetner by diabetics.

Asparagus, *Asparagus officinalis,* was, like the globe artichoke, another plant brought in from the wilds by the assiduous gardeners of that fertile region around the Nile and the Indus. Two thousand years later its priapic appearance had earned it its lustful, tumescent Greek name *asparagos*. The Romans introduced it to Europe. (Pliny reportedly bought three giant asparagus heads that weighed around half a kilogram.) The English diarist Samuel Pepys (1633–1703) reported buying 'a bundle of sparrow-grass' in London's Fenchurch Street for one shilling and sixpence and growers and market traders alike still

Fifty Tales from the Kitchen Garden

sometimes refer to it as grass. It was always regarded as a vegetable extravagance: 'The asparaginous class of esculents may be considered as comparatively one of luxury,' wrote Loudon in the 1800s. 'It occupies a large proportion of the gentleman's garden, often an eighth part; but does not enter into that of the cottager.' He recommended the grower devote 'five square poles of ground, planted with 1600 plants' for a yield of 'six to eight score heads daily.'

Some kitchen gardeners find it difficult to grow, yet in the wild *Asparagus officinalis* proved to be a determined coloniser, settling its fat little roots down just about everywhere from Morocco to Manchester. As economically important to Venetian traders as their home-blown glass, (farmers around Bassano were busy with their asparagus beds in the 1500s), asparagus was carried over to the Americas by the early settlers. It made little impact on the American diet until it was canned and turned into a cheap (but poor) substitute for fresh asparagus.

Other vegetables raised in the Nile and Indus region included the beetroot, carrot, celery, pea and turnip. The beetroot, *Beta vulgaris,* was growing here 4,000 years ago. While the Greeks ate the leaf of the beet, the Romans enjoyed its swollen red root, which explains why the English ate their 'Roman beet' in Tudor times. In 1597 John Gerard wrote of the 'great red Beete or Romaine Beete': 'the beautiful roote which is to be preferred before the leaves, as well in beautie as in goodnesse'. Given a good feed, he claimed beetroot could grow to 12 feet (3.5 metres). By 1656 the beetroot, now being grown by the gardener and plant hunter John Tradescant the younger, was referred to as the *'beet rave* or beet-radish' from the French *betterave.*

A direct descendent of the beetroot, the mangle, mangold or mangle-wurzle, still grown as a prize exhibit at agricultural shows, started life in the German Rhineland as a chance hybrid between the beetroot and a white-stemmed chard. The great gnarled roots were fed to cattle, but not before they had been lifted and weathered in a clamp long enough for their natural toxins to have leached away.

The carrot, *Daucus carota,* was a younger vegetable than the beetroot, but only by a thousand years or so. Unlike the potato it was welcomed into the British kitchen garden of the 1500s: 'Sowe Carrets in your Gardens, and humbly praise God for them, as for a singular and great blessing.' So instructed Richard Gardiner in his 1599 *Profitable Instructions for the Manuring, Sowing and Planting of Kitchen Gardens* (manuring in this instance meaning cultivating).

Three and a half centuries later the propaganda character of Dr Carrot was believed to be making a significant contribution to the British war effort. The nightly blackout, designed to hide its towns and villages from enemy bombing raids, tested the nocturnal vision of its citizens and the carrot, packed with vitamins which benefited the optical nerves, was promoted as a natural aid for those fumbling their way home in the dark. 'Eat carrots and leafy green or yellow vegetables...rich in Vitamin "A", essential for night sight,' read one poster aimed at US soldiers: 'Night Sight can mean Life or Death.' The claims were exaggerated and led to an estimated surplus of 100,000 tons of carrots in 1942.

The carrot of choice was an orangey red. This, however, was but one of a rainbow selection of coloured carrots ranging from scarlet and purple to white and yellow. The Romans referred to them as both *daucus* and *carota,* (Carl Linnaeus accorded them both names), and while their conquering legions almost certainly brought them through Europe, the European tribes of Saxons, Celts, Angles and Vikings seem to have ignored the beneficial carrot for a thousand years. It was left to the Moors

Fifty Tales from the Kitchen Garden

to re-introduce the purple carrot from the Middle East in the 900s. The Spanish Moors were growing carrots by the 1100s, the Germans and Dutch by the 1300s, the English by the 1400s and the American Virginians in the 1600s when colonists first sowed the seed there - and let loose the wild carrot that spread across the continent. The Americans and the Chinese would eventually become the world's major carrot growers, but it was industrious Dutch gardeners who, in 1720, produced the Long Orange Dutch cultivar, the prototype for the modern varieties.

It was Moorish gardeners too who were responsible for developing celeriac (*Apium graveolens var. rapaceum*), the swollen-rooted vegetable that became such a popular plant in central and eastern Europe and carried the now forgotten alternative name of Dutch or Hamburg parsley. But true celery, *Apium graveolens,* was yet another vegetable that emerged from the Indus plains 4,000 years ago. By Roman times there was talk of the little pot herb called *apium* being used to flavour fish, as a garnish in sauces and, strangely, as a decorative head gear for their champion games players. But it was left to future generations of Italians to develop the *sedano*, the crisp, thick stalked celery that we eat today. It may have been introduced to northern Europe by an Italian, Giacomo Castelvetro, who, living in exile in England in 1614, described how to grow and prepare it. When it reached America with the early settlers, like the carrot it bolted for the wild and spread far and wide.

The pea, *Pisum sativum*, was another vegetable believed to be rooted in the fertile Middle East. (Peas and vetches – also members of the pea family - were standard fare in most early civilisations.) Four thousand years later the Greeks were enjoying their bizéli. Subsequently the Romans introduced their *pisum* to the rest of Europe. Early peas had coloured flowers and small pods and were grown as a field crop, but gradually the white

107

flowered garden varieties with larger peas were developed. Thomas Hill in his *Gardeners Labyrinth* of 1577 proposed successional sowings of 'Rounseval pease' in spring, the name said to be derived from the large seeded peas named after Roncesvalles Abbey, the collegiate church and resting place for weary pilgrims on route to Santiago de Compostela. (The reference is obscure: Roncesvalles was the site of the legendary battle in which Roland, or Orlando as the Italians called him, died. The much-respected Roland was a giant among men at eight feet (2.4 metres) tall, while a rouncival was a big woman.)

A century later the rounseval peas were known as marrowfat peas, the essential ingredient in the traditional northern England dish, mushy peas. Dried peas ground into flour and mixed with wheat or rye were also used to make bread. They would be soaked overnight and turned into pease porridge or pease pudding. In Scotland pea flour, known as peasemeal, would be mixed with water and milk, or whey, and baked on a griddle to make bannocks.

The habit of eating under-ripe peas fresh from the pod arose, not amongst purchasers of the 20th century freezer packs, but in the 1600s during a craze at the court of Louis X1V who had a passion for *petit pois*. It was a passion shared later by an English poet and an American president. The poet was William Wordsworth (1770–1850) - his sister Dorothy noted in her diary whenever her brother set off to stake his peas and of how he had to lie down afterwards, exhausted by his exertions. Another prize pea grower, although he had slaves to do the hard work for him, was the US president Thomas Jefferson. A keen gardener, Jefferson liked to compete with his neighbours to grow the first crop of peas fit for the plate. By staggering his planting and growing at least fifteen different varieties of English peas, Jefferson expected fresh peas to be served on the dinner

Fifty Tales from the Kitchen Garden

plate at his Virginia farm, Monticello from mid May to mid July. But a Mr George Divers usually grew the first crop and had the privilege of throwing a celebration dinner. Jefferson finally beat Mr Divers. However, in a masterful show of modesty, he kept the news to himself and dined with his supposedly victorious neighbour as usual. 'It will be more agreeable to our friend to think he never fails,' Jefferson explained to his family.

Although the pea had been brought into cultivation and improved in the Middle East, it was one of the earliest domesticated plants. Bronze Age families, for example, were eating peas five thousand years ago. Could it lay claim to be one of the world's first garden vegetables? Three other vegetables cultivated in what was the Middle East could also be considered as odds-on favourites: the lettuce, the onion and the leek.

In the 1800s an Edinburgh doctor was marketing his *Lactucarium*, an 'opium juice' made from lettuce: the name of the lettuce, *Lactuca sativa,* recalls the fact that the Romans too used it as a mild narcotic. Their lettuce exuded a bitter sap or latex which, having similar properties to laudanum, promised a good night's sleep - the name came from the Roman *lactuca* or milk.

However the lettuce, a relative of the chicory family, was brought into cultivation far earlier than Roman times. Cos or 'Roman' lettuces were pictured on five thousand year old Egyptian tomb reliefs (although they earned the term Roman or their French name *laitue romaine* when they were brought to Avignon by the papal court of the 1300s). Theories abound as to why the English should have named the 'cos' lettuce after the Greek island of Kos, but, since Kos was the birthplace of the physician Hippocrates, it may have been to mark the medicinal qualities of the vegetable. An Italian recipe from 1614 recommended quartering the lettuce, dressing the quarters with oil, salt and

 Bill Laws

pepper and then roasting them over a charcoal grill before eating them sprinkled with orange juice. With butterheads, crispheads and cut-and-come again varieties there are now as many different lettuces as there are months in the year. It is nothing new: lettuces were being harvested all year round in Britain back in the 1800s.

The second contender for the oldest garden vegetable is the onion. To 'know your onions' is to know all. The Indian Brahmin knew the onion well enough to avoid it, and anything else 'arising from impurity,' all together. The onion, *Allium cepa,* is a member of the lily family that probably originated in the central Asia regions, although no one knows for sure. Spread by traders throughout the world, it was part of the staple diet in Greek and Roman times, the latter, possibly, giving it the name *unio* for singularity.

The leek, *Allium porrum,* like the onion a member of the lily family, may be one of the world's most ancient vegetables, but it is certainly one of the main ingredients in what may prove to be the world's oldest recipe. A 4,000-year-old inscribed Babylonian tablet suggests using crushed leeks to spice up a lamb stew. The Greeks called the leek *prasa,* the Arabs *kurrats* and the Romans, who brought them into northern Europe, *porrum*. Why the Celtic Welsh, who successfully held out against the invading Romans, should have adopted the leek as their national emblem is something of a national mystery, but given their love of song and oration, it may have been associated with the leek's throat-soothing, mucilaginous qualities: the Roman Nero, derided as a *porrophagus* or leek-eater, ate leeks to improve his voice. Since he also invented the art of sycophantic applause, his success may be thrown into question.

24. Out of India

Two important vegetables, the aubergine and the cucumber, came into cultivation from the Indian sub continent. The Indian aubergine, *Solanum melongena*, is a member of the Solanum family along with deadly nightshade, *Atropa belladonna*. The aubergine was not welcomed when first it arrived in England, partly because of its fearsome family connections and partly because it was blamed for a succession of ailments from piles, halitosis and liver obstructions to a poor complexion and, ultimately, leprosy. But, suggested John Parkinson in the 1600s, it was perfectly safe if boiled first in vinegar.

In Sanskrit it was *vatin-gana,* a wind killer, but it was also known as a melongene, Jew's apple, mad apple, brinjal and egg plant (early varieties were small, white, egg-like fruit rather than the deep purple of modern varieties). Its Hindustani name was *Bungan*, which became the Arabic *al-badingan*. When the Moslems swept through Egypt and North Africa in the 700s and replanted the local vineyards with their own vegetables, they brought it into Spain (the Spanish still call it *berenjena*), Sicily and the Languedoc region of France.

The cucumber, *Cucumis sativus,* came out of the foothills of the eastern Himalayas. This runs counter to the claim of William

Tyndale who, when he translated the bible in the 1500s (he was strangled and burned as a heretic for his efforts), asserted in the Book of Isaiah that the daughter of Zion lodged 'in a garden of cucumbers'. Grown in England as early as the 14th century (in the days of the much married King Henry VIII), the cucumber was regarded as an enemy of lust by the 16th century garden author Thomas Hill. He also claimed that a thunderstorm would cause the cucumber to bend. The cucumber was so called after the Old French *cocombre*. However the 'little wild cucumber' of the West Indies, although related to the cucumber and better known as the gherkin, *Cucumis anguria,* was carried from southwest Africa to the West Indies in the 1600s with the slave trade. It earned its name from the Dutch *augurkje*.

The Roman Emperor Tiberius had a particular passion for the *cucumis* and the Romans created fantastical shaped cucumbers by encasing the young fruits in wood, wicker or clay casts. There was to be none of this nonsense in the Victorian kitchen where the cook insisted upon long, straight fruit, achieved by hanging lantern-like glass cylinders around the growing cucumber.

25. Out of Rome

Julius Caesar led his conquering Romans against the Gallic tribes fifty years before the start of the Christian calendar. By the time he finished modern day France and Belgium had become part of the great Roman republic, its colonising citizens bringing with them from Italy their civic buildings, villas, roads and their favourite vegetables. The wild cabbage, *Brassica oleracea,* for example has uncertain origins, but it was Romans who nurtured it in northern Europe along with their parsnips and turnips. (In Britain, after the fall of the Roman empire many roots crops were largely forgotten and it was left to the wholesome cabbage and onion to fill a hungry gap of 1,000 years until the Renaissance.) A polymorphic plant is one that, chameleon-like, can take on different forms. The cabbage is a polymorphic triumph and there are six main cultivars: non-heading kales, heading cabbages, swollen stemmed kohlrabi, Brussels sprouts, broccoli and cauliflower. But leave them growing together for long enough and all six will cross pollinate and gradually revert to their wild cabbage cousin.

Each of the brassicas seems to have developed as a regional favourite. Brussel sprouts, for example, were first recorded in Belgium around 1750, hence the name. 'At Brussels they are sometimes served at table with a sauce composed of vinegar, butter, and nutmeg, poured upon them hot after they have been boiled,' reported an incredulous Loudon. In northeastern Europe, *choucroute* or *sauerkraut*, made from finely shredded cabbage leaves pickled with juniper berries and sea salt for three weeks in stone crocks, became a favourite. The cauliflower (what the American writer Mark Twain dismissed as 'a cabbage with a college education') was brought into Spain in the 1400s by the Moors and was growing in London a century later. The broccolis were always an Italian favourite. Phillip Miller described it as Italian asparagus in 1724 and it was Italian immigrants who took their beloved broccoli to America.

Kohlrabi, possibly the vegetable described as a 'Corinthian turnip' by the Roman Pliny The Elder, was promoted as a novelty vegetable in Victorian times. Jane Grigson in *The Vegetable Book* of 1978 took a less-said-the-better approach to kohlrabi: 'there are better vegetables than kohlrabi. And worse.' Which may explain why much of the kohlrabi grown in Britain was fed to cattle.

The old English name for the turnip, *wort*, belies its ancestry as a member of the brassica family. In Ireland the Gaelic *neep* was an important crop, sown in drills, which ran the length of the field, alongside the potato ridges. The seed, hand sown, would be dipped in highly toxic red lead to protect it against birds.

The Romans also enjoyed their *pastinaca* or parsnip. The Frenchman still enjoys *le panais*, the German his *pastinake*, the Russian his *pasternak* and the Italian his *pastinaca*, since it was the Romans who popularised the parsnip, *Pastinaca sativa,* in these countries. The English linked the French *pasnaie* with the turnip or neep, and John Gerard gave it his qualified support: 'the Parsneps nourish more than do the Turneps or the Carrots, and the nourishment is somewhat thicker; but

Fifty Tales from the Kitchen Garden

not faultie nor bad.' The parsnip sweetened in the ground, its starch being converted to sugar by frost action. It was eaten on Ash Wednesday during Lent, cooked to accompany salt cod. Thomas Hill in his *Gardener's Labyrinth* recommended sowing 'parsnep' in well-manured ground in high summer for eating in Lent the following year. Used to make wine and to sweeten cakes in the days when honey was the major source of sugar, its high sugar and starch content has ensured it has been grown in the kitchen garden ever since.

Curiously, when the parsnip reached Virginia in 1609 it was held in high esteem by the Native Americans, but largely ignored by the North Americans. Perhaps this was because the Native Americans in the southwest and Mexico were accustomed to making a meal out of the baked, ground root of the wild parsnip. In Britain meanwhile, and so long as north European Protestants still regarded the potato as only fit for 'pigs and papists', the parsnip was the preferred accompaniment to roast beef.

Another seasonal accompaniment were broad beans, *Vicia faba*, which, like the faba, field, winter, tick or horse bean had been cultivated since biblical times. Ancient broad bean-like seeds 8,500 years old have been found in the Middle East and the seeds probably reached northern Europe in the hand luggage of the Roman centurion. Originally a black bean, the broad bean was a valuable crop since the seed could be eaten fresh or dried and the plant's nitrogen-fixing qualities endeared it to the gardener. It was such a prize crop that, by the Middle Ages, the crime of stealing beans from open fields carried the death penalty. The bean had its own revenge for it had a fierce reputation for flatulence: 'Broad beans are very nutritious, but are not easily digested and should not be given to invalids,' warned the cautious author of one kitchen encyclopaedia. The poet William Butler Yeats was untroubled by its notoriety:

 Bill Laws

I will arise and go now, and go to Innisfree,
And a small cabin build there, of clay and wattles made;
Nine bean-rows will I have there, a hive for the honey bee,
And live alone in the bee-loud glade he wrote in *The Lake Isle of Innisfree*, published in 1893.

Exercising poetic licence, Yeats did not mention whether he preferred the broad bean or one of the many garden beans that had originated on the other side of the world - America.

26. Out of America

European gardeners owe a debt of gratitude to the American Indians for their protein-rich maize, squash, potatoes and beans. The new American civilisation owes its very existence to them.

Forty years before Yeats penned his poem, that contemplative gardener Henry David Thoreau was planning his own Indian bean patch, on the shores of Walden Pond at Concord, Massachusetts. 'What shall I learn of beans or beans of me? I cherish them, I hoe them, early and late I have an eye to them and this is my days work.'

Thoreau, however, did not eat his beans but sold them to buy rice. He was growing 'the common small white bush bean,' one of more than 50 varieties of *Phaseolus*, all originating from the Americas and embracing French, navy, flageolet, snap, *haricot vert*, scarlet or runner bean (*Phaseolus coccineus*), and the Lima or butter bean (*Phaseolus lunatus*).

The Webbs Seed catalogue for 1888 noted: 'The Kidney Bean, *Phaseolus vulgaris,* has been cultivated for a considerable time, but there is uncertainty as to whether it was known in Europe before the discovery of America, where the genus is strongly represented.' It was not. The kidney bean, which still grows wild in South America, came into Europe in the 16th century stashed alongside the Spanish *conquistadores'* captured gold. When the scarlet flowered runner bean reached the royal gardens of England during the reign of Charles I it was grown purely for its pretty flowers. It was not until the early 1700s that Philip Miller, who ran the Chelsea Physic in London, advocated cooking and eating the green pods.

Spanish *conquistadores* also brought the capsicum pepper, *Capsicum frutescens* to their mother country in the 1500s. They called it the *pimento* and the Italians took the *pepperone* to heart, making it an indispensable ingredient in their kitchen recipes. The capsicum, when dried and crushed, was popular elsewhere in Europe because it served as an acceptable substitute for pepper at a time when true black peppercorns were proving too expensive for the kitchen table.

When Columbus brought home yet another 'new' Latin American crop, its old Mexican name, *cintli*, was replaced with the Spanish word *maiz* instead. (Columbus had discovered the crop growing in Cuba where it was known by the local Indians as *maisi*).

Zea *mays*, a member of the grass family, was to become one of the world's most popular - and most important - crops. Variously known as corn, sweet corn, Indian corn, mealies, corn-on-the cob and popcorn, it was originally cultivated by native American Indians and not only sustained the Toltecs, Aztecs, Mayas and Incas, but also the new immigrant American civilisation: in 1810 the population of America was around six million. Largely fed on maize, it had risen to 94 million a century later.

Within a century of reaching Spain, maize had spread across the globe. William Cobbett spoke of it growing in Britain by 1803 and although it was, and still is, fed to cows, it became, in the form of cornflakes or corn on the cob, a foodie's favourite. Maize also generated its own legendary figures. There was the Mexican goddess of plenty, Centeotl, and the American Indian Mondamin, a green giant who was killed and buried by Hiawatha. The maize plant that rose up from Mondamin's grave saved Hiawatha's people from a winter's starvation. Because the sugar in the corn starts to convert to starch the moment it is picked, sweet corn is best when picked and eaten fresh from the kitchen garden: 'the principle of the lathe is adopted in eating them,' explained Edward Bunyard helpfully in the 1930s.

Bunyard was also an enthusiastic supporter of another American import, the marrow. 'We may use it for jam, pies, soup, etc., its merit being its placid acceptance of all flavours.'

Marrows, pumpkins and squashes are all members of the cucurbita (gourd) genus which originated in the Americas and had arrived in Europe within 50 years of Columbus' voyages. Seeds have been found on ancient Mexican sites and the cucurbits formed a staple part of the diet, along with maize and beans, of the Native American Indians living on the east coast of America. When the first Pilgrim Fathers landed at Cape Cod, Massachusetts in 1620 those who survived starvation were rescued by Patuxet Indians who taught them how to grow pumpkins among their corn, burying a herring beneath the crop as fertiliser. In October 1621 the settlers ate a ceremonial meal of boiled pumpkins as a thanksgiving for their survival. Although the recipe has been improved, the custom has continued.

The name squash came from the Algonquin Indians and the pumpkin from the Greek, and later Old French, *poumpon.* In terms of alternative uses, the cucurbita are the world's most versatile vegetable: in their different forms they have served as cups, bottles, the back-scrubbing loofah, soaps, household ornaments, yak fodder and, in the form of the *kamandalam,* the Hindu hermit's precious water pot.

While we are used to a pale- or yellow-fleshed potato, *Solanum tuberosum,* those growing still in the wilds of South America, from where they originated, range in colour from yellow and red through to purple and black. The horticultural Incas built terraces and aqueducts to feed their potatoes, which were cultivated as a storage crop and which complemented the maize, grown at lower levels. (Growing potatoes for seed in a cold, blight-free climate benefited the tubers and explains why Scotland traditionally produced the best seed potatoes in Britain.)

The Spanish explorer, Gonzalo Jiménez de Quesada, is claimed to be one of the first Europeans to have encountered the fertile spud around 1536. The Spanish discovered the truffle-like tubers, or *'turmas de tierra'* as they called them, in the tropical forests of Columbia's northern Andes. From here they were almost certainly carried back to Spain and up the river Guadalquivir to Seville in 1573. (There is some confusion here as the sweet potato, *Ipomoea batatas*, which had been discovered in Haiti by the explorer Columbus, was also being imported to southern Spain around this time.) The potato travelled on to Italy as *tartufflo,* and into France as *cartoufle,* but it arrived in England in the 1590s by a different route and with a different name.

John Gerard mentions the 'potatoe of Virginia' in 1597. Gerard, a London barber-surgeon, was an enthusiastic gardener who not only managed several of London's society gardens, but also looked after his own plot of ground in Holborn. Here he grew 'all the rare simples' and 'strange trees, herbes, rootes, plants, flowers, and other such rare things.' When in 1596 he catalogued his plants, the year before his famous Herbal was published, the potato appeared in the inventory. When the second issue of the Herbal was published, Gerard dedicated it to Sir Walter

Fifty Tales from the Kitchen Garden

Raleigh, who, some say, introduced the first pinch of tobacco and the first potato to Britain.

'To England the potatoe found its way ... being brought from Virginia by the colonists sent out by Sir Walter Raleigh in 1584, and who returned in July 1586, and "probably," according to Sir Joseph Banks, " brought with them the potatoe",' explained John Loudon in 1824.

The story goes that Raleigh came by both potato and tobacco through another English knight, Sir Francis Drake. Drake, who had been battling with the Spaniards in the Caribbean, sailed for England after collecting some provisions including potatoes at Cartagena, Columbia. Drake also picked up a group of Virginian colonists who had had enough of the hard life and wanted to return home. Drake's ship, The Golden Hind, berthed in Cork in southern Ireland, leaving a few of his potatoes with Raleigh who grew them on at his Youghal home in County Cork. Raleigh's gardener is said to have sent the poisonous potato fruit to the kitchen rather than the root. The rest arrived in Britain, possibly in Lancashire, but Gerard, confusing the returning colonists with the vegetable, cultivated them under the name *Battata virginiana,* the Virginian potato.

The tomato, *Lycopersicum esculentum,* like the potato, came from South America. The ancient ancestors of the fat, red tomato grew wild on the riverbanks of Peru and Ecuador and grows there still. When it spread into Central America and Mexico resourceful American Indians brought it into cultivation. Spanish *conquistadores* came across what the Indians called *tomatl* and shipped the fruit back to Seville from where it travelled to Italy. In 1544 one Italian writer recommended cooking the tomato 'like an eggplant - fried in oil with salt and pepper.' He called the fruit *'mala aurea'* or golden apple. Linnaeus classified it as *L. esculentum,* but its supposed links with mandrake

(*Mandragon autumnalis*), a notorious narcotic which reportedly shrieked when pulled from the ground, branded the tomato a dangerous fruit, good only for table decoration. 'In Spaine and those hot regions they used to eat prepared and boil'd with pepper, salt and oil; but they yield very little nourishment to the body and the same naught and corrupt,' explained John Gerard. John Parkinson described it in terms with which those prejudiced against the tomato would agree: it was, he wrote, 'full of slimie juice and waterie pulp.'

In Europe the tomato became what the French called *pomme d'amour* or love apple, a reference to its supposed aphrodisiac qualities. Its powers to promote promiscuity earned it yet another name - mad or rage apple. Although the American president Thomas Jefferson was content to grow them in his Monticello garden in the 1780s, the tomato clearly needed further promotion. In 1820, Robert Gibbon Johnson helped it along by publicly eating a basket of tomatoes on the steps of the courthouse in Salem, New Jersey to dispel the myth that the tomato was poisonous. The argument over whether it was a fruit or a vegetable (and thus earns a place in this book) was settled by an American court of law. John Nix, seeking to avoid a 10% tax on vegetables imported to the US, claimed the tomato was a fruit. The Supreme Court in 1893 ruled that, while the tomato, like the cucumber and squash, was a 'fruit of a vine,' these were all 'in the common language of the people, ... vegetables which are grown in the kitchen garden.'

27. Out in the Cold

One vegetable that was almost lost to the kitchen garden is the skirret (*Sium sisarum*), a perennial tap-rooted plant that originated in China and was grown in Europe for over four centuries. In Scotland the skirret was cultivated under the name of crummock. The gentleman gardener John Worlidge described skirrets as 'the sweetest, whitest, and most pleasant of roots' in 1682; William Shakespeare (1564–1616) makes mentions of them 80 years earlier in his *Merry Wives of Windsor*; and the Elizabethan poet, Michael Drayton (1563–1631) commended them in his poem published in 1612, *Poly-Olbion*: 'The Skirret (which some way) in sallats [salads] stirs the blood'. Although still eaten in China and Japan, the root had disappeared from one English kitchen garden calendar by 1876. Seasoned allotment holders were accustomed to finding the starry flowers of escaped specimens decorating the paths between their plots, but it still caused a stir when kitchen gardeners at the royal Hampton Court palace decided to restore its fortunes in 2016.

The swede, on the other hand, slipped into a culinary wilderness in mid 1900s Britain as a result of cheap school dinners and a heavy reliance on the vegetable during the Second World War. Jane Grigson in her *Vegetable Book* judged 'the watery orange slush ... unredeemable by drainage or butter.' In the root bed the swede is a close cousin of the turnip and was commonly confused with it in the vegetable taxonomy. When the swede was taken to America it arrived with its Swedish name of ram's root or *rotbagga*. The turnip, from the Latin *napus,* became in the 1500s the *neep* in Britain, but when, on Burn's Night, a haggis was put on the hob along with *neeps*, the *neeps* were swedes and not turnips.

28. What's in a Name

The curious names of some vegetables shine a light on their histories: perhaps when returning Crusaders brought seeds of the Persian *ispanai* or *isfanai* home, it was mispronounced as our spinach. But did the French bean really originate in France? Did the eating of cucumbers cause such offence that someone had to invent a burpless variety? And why do Americans grow zucchini and the British courgettes?

The bean provides a starting point for some linguistic origins, and confusions, of vegetables. Take the dwarf kidney bean also known as the French bean and in France *haricot vert,* a tender bean eaten pods and all, and *haricot jaune,* podded and harvested for the seed. *Haricot* comes from its Aztec name, *ayacotl,* but it became the French bean because it was the Gallic gardeners who cultivated it. The French *flageolet* bean was so called either because it looked like a flute or *flageolet* or was a corruption of *Phaseolus.* (It was the French, too, who gave the 'Hasty' pea, a large and early variety, its name - from *hâtif* or early.)

Phaseolus, the Latin name for a small, fast-sailing craft, referred to the canoe-like shape of the bean pod while the kidney bean itself earned its name from its similarity to that part of the body.

The climbing bean was known to gardeners at the English court of Charles 1 as the 'runner' bean. It had been collected in Virginia, USA by the King's gardener, John Tradescant, and given to the monarch as a decorative plant. But back in its homeland it became known as the string bean, a reference to the stringy seams that run down each side of the pod.

When the *Phaseolus* began to supplement the old fashioned field, Celtic and broad bean (all varieties of *Vicia faba*) John Gerard spoke with surprise of being able to eat them 'cods and all.' Favourite varieties in the early 1800s included the Windsor, so-called by Huguenot gardeners simply because Windsor happened to be a profitable place to grow them, and the Mazagan. 'Sow the first crop of early (pea) varieties, rolling the seed in red lead, and filling the drills half full over the peas with chopped furze' (bracken) 'or chopped barley chaff. Sow dwarf Peas in pot. Plant Mazagan Bean, and treat in the same way,' advised the *Illustrated Guide for Amateur Gardeners* of 1876.

Mazagan was a small Portuguese settlement on the coast of Morocco and seed from the settlement promised to produce a well-flavoured, early crop. The English naturalist, Reverend Gilbert White, was already well ahead of the pack when he wrote in his *Garden Kalendar* on November 2 1754: 'Started ten rows of Mazagan-beans (never planted in England) in the field garden.'

As for the potato, another vegetable championed by the good vicar of Selbourne in Hampshire, it was the Peruvians who referred to it as *papas* and hence its one time French name, *la papas des Péruviens*. In Wales the potato became *pytatws* and in the Scottish vernacular *tatties,* which sounds more like the Spanish name for the sweet potato, *batatas.*

Another linguistic throwback concerns the 'ridge' cucumber, so called for its habit of climbing over the old-fashioned ridges in the ridge and channel system of vegetable growing. The cucumber, especially in the raw, was viewed with some suspicion by English Victorian gentleman who preferred it stewed and served in a white sauce. The arrival of a thinner-skinned and sweeter 'Burpless' variety, calmed all fears of an accidental, tea-time belch and the uncooked cucumber went on to become the staple sandwich filling at vicarage tea parties.

And finally, why do Americans whose 'squash' seeds were taken to Europe in the 1500s now find themselves eating 'zucchini'? It was the Italian immigrants who reintroduced the courgette to its place of origin, along with their name for it. In France the zucchini remained a courgette, from the word *courge* or gourd and the British, setting aside their traditional differences, adopted the word courgette too. That was until the courgette grew to a monstrous size when, just to be awkward, it became a 'marrow'.

29. The Secret of Selling Seeds

The seed is the beginning of all things. '*Germination* is that act of operation of the vegetative principle by which the embryo is extricated from its envelopes, and converted into a plant. This is universally the first part of the process of vegetation. For it may be regarded as an indubitable fact, that all plants spring originally from seed.'

So wrote John Loudon in his *Encyclopaedia of Gardening*. It was published in 1822 shortly after the seed merchants, Messers Sutton and Son, distributed a printed list of the seeds they sold. It was not the nation's first seed catalogue - seed sellers and nursery people had been advertising their wares in newspapers and magazines for a half a century or more - but it was the first to offer the kitchen gardener a current price list and useful advice on when and how to plant their vegetable seed. It was also the first of many devices designed to ensure that a well-thumbed copy of the seed catalogue survived the growing season and was still on hand in winter when it was time to reorder seeds.

At first seed companies relied on the fine and often inspirational line drawings of their artists and the enthusiasm of their

Fifty Tales from the Kitchen Garden

copywriters to sell their wares: 'With great satisfaction we now introduce a new White Kidney which we have had under trial for several years. It was raised by the late Mr. Clark, the raiser of our Magnum Bonum, Abundance, and other heavy cropping varieties, and combines the high quality of Victoria in its best days with the productiveness of White Elephant. The yield has astonished experienced growers to whom we sent small parcels for trial.'

The subject of this entry in a Sutton's seed catalogue was the potato Sutton Perfection. Sutton's and other catalogue editors were quick to learn the value of publishing testimonials alongside advertisements for 'The Student Parsnep,' the 'Redtop Mousetail Turnip' and the 'Prince of Wales, a heavy cropping Pea, which has long been popular with amateurs and cottagers.'

'I have cut Cucumbers from your Berks Champion three weeks earlier than any of my neighbours,' boasted the Reverend J.R. Barlow of Pertenhall, Kimbolton with a singular lack of modesty in a Sutton catalogue for 1881.

The people who paid the seed bills were the gentry, even if it was their head gardeners who ordered them, and the catalogues could be both obsequious - 'Gentlemen are respectfully invited to have price from us before ordering elsewhere' - and charitable:

'From your beautiful and valuable Amateur's Guide, I have made a common labouring lad into a most excellent practical Gardener,' revealed a Mrs Parsons of The Castle, Buttevant, County Cork. 'I do not see anywhere nicer work or so good things as he grows, and all his education has been from one of your Guides.'

Colour printing processes transformed the appearance - but not the prose - of the seed catalogues in the second half of the 1800s just as the American seed market, previously a profitable source of income for European seed growers, developed its own seed industry. In their battles for supremacy, the 800 or so US seed merchants proved to be innovative marketeers. There were free gifts of seeds and more testimonials: 'The package of Vandergaw Cabbage you sent me did much better than the Large Late Flat Dutch.' There were promotions, price wars and prizes: 'We offer, for 1888, CASH PRIZES OF $25.00 and $10.00 for the two largest onions raised from seed purchased of us this year - the onions, or reliable affidavits of their weights, to be sent to us before Nov. 1st,' promised the authors of the Burpee catalogue, which in 1888 ran to 128 pages, most of them devoted to vegetables.

There were slick slogans. 'Seeds That Yield are Sold by Field' was the catch phrase of Henry Field who started out on horseback selling seed around Shenandoah. By the 1920s Field, a plain-speaking man, had set up the Farmer Friendly Radio Station to sell his wares. 'Cut out book English and talk modern United States,' he instructed his employees in their battle with his competitor, Earl May, who ran the town's rival station.

In France meanwhile, one of the nation's most senior seed firms, Vilmorin, devised a clever strategy for selling their products: the picture. The company was based on an old family firm, Le Febvre, run by Pierre Geoffroy. In 1782 Geoffroy's daughter Claude, or Mâitresse Grainière (the Seed Mistress) as she was known, and her husband Pierre Andrieux, botanist to Louis XIV, opened a shop on the Mégisserie Quay in Paris. The business, later run by their daughter and her husband, Philippe-Victoire De Vilmorin, became Vilmorin-Andrieux and later, Vilmorin Co. Responsible for introducing the field beetroot and 'rutabaga' or swede to France, Philippe-Victoire was also a good publicist. He not only commissioned watercolours to illustrate their catalogues and seed packets (Vilmorin vegetable posters would become highly desirable collectables), but also ordered a collection

Fifty Tales from the Kitchen Garden

of artificial vegetables to be exhibited at the Paris Universal Exhibition in 1855. Made of plaster, each was a perfect replica in weight and colour of the vegetable itself.

Seed sales people learned to be economical with the truth, picturing on their seed packets and catalogues magnificently exaggerated versions of their produce. The underlying aim was, as it has become and ever more will be, to appeal to the aspirational gardener.

It was not always so. Plain vegetable seed was being sold, without any trimmings, from The Strand in London in the late 1600s. The garden historian John Harvey has traced at least five nurseries in and around the capital at that time, the largest, London and Wise, occupying 100 acres of what would later become the site of the Albert Hall and the South Kensington Museum.

The sale of vegetable seed, measured by the bushel and hundredweight, was a lucrative business then worth over half a million pounds ($623,000) a year. While it was concentrated on the south east, each region contributed its own regional specialities to what Loudon called the Middlesex seed market 'held twice a week in a large roofed space in Mark-lane. The purchasers are the London retailers, or the wholesale dealers for their country customers.' Kent gardeners brought their radish, kidney beans, turnips, 'toker or Sandwich beans' and onions; Berkshire men brought their cabbages and white skinned or Reading onion seeds while in Worcestershire and Warwickshire the market gardeners took their seeds of white onions, asparagus, cucumber and carrot to the Birmingham markets. (In Leicestershire, Loudon noted, 'the farmers, tho often rich, have seldom good gardens.')

Seed was also sold by stall holders, costermongers and barrow boys at country markets. Those who chose not to buy, or could not afford to do so, carefully collected and stored their own seed in mouse-proof draws and rat-proof safes, despite the advice of garden writers such as Shirley Hibberd: 'the professional seed-grower will beat you nine times out of ten... and if you deal with none but respectable seedsmen, and avoid the cheap rubbish that is vended in odd corners, you will save a good deal of labour.'

Thomas Tusser, however, was in favour of trading seed locally: 'One seed for another to make an exchange
With fellowy neighbours seemeth not strange,' he suggested in 1580. Ideally, home seed was selected, not from some stunted individual that had been missed during the harvest, but from the earliest, healthiest and most vigorous vegetables. Carrots and cabbages, which formed seed in their second year, were lifted whole in their first autumn. The carrots, after their foliage was cut back, were buried or clamped in beds of peat or sand. The brassicas, their root balls still intact, were tenderly wrapped in cloth and hung from the rafters of a dry shed where they held their breath until spring when they could be replanted and their seed harvested when it was set. Alternatively, the cabbage could be buried outside. 'Market gardeners and many private individuals, raise seed for their own use,' wrote Loudon. 'Some of the handsomest cabbages... are dug up in autumn, and sunk in the ground to the head; early next summer a flower-stem appears, which is followed by an abundance of seed.' Loudon offered even more exacting detail: 'It is mentioned in Bastien, that the seed-growers of Aubervilliers have learned by experience, that seed gathered from the middle flower-stem produces plants which will be fit for use a fortnight earlier.'

Well ripened and dried, the seed would keep for six to eight years, he added, confirming the conviction that seed improved with age. For example, three to four years was judged ideal for

Fifty Tales from the Kitchen Garden

cucumber seed while soaking the seed in sheep's milk or mead (the alcoholic drink made from fermented honey) prevented the fruit from turning bitter.

Success was guaranteed when seed was 'sown dry and set wet'. The failure of seed to set true or perform like its parent was blamed on indifferent or poor soil. But once Carl Linnaeus revealed that cross pollination between different varieties of the same species could cause problems, seeds people began to exploit this characteristic to improve or 'enoble' vegetable seeds. In 1888 for example, Webbs' Seeds announced the arrival of their new, cross-breed pea, the Wordsley Wonder: 'This wonderful Pea is the result of crosses between Advancer, Little Gem, and Prizetaker, and whilst possessing all the good qualities of the two former varieties, it has both the constitution and productiveness of the latter. As a first early Pea for large gardens, it is unequalled, and its convenient height and cropping properties render it indispensable to the amateur.'

So the practise of improving seed, although not necessarily for the good of the gardener continued until, in the 1960s, the F1 hybrids, which had been developed in the 1920s, began to emerge. The F of F1 stood for *filia,* Latin for daughter, and the seeds promised to revolutionise the kitchen garden, developed as they were by crossing two selected lines to produce vigorous growth from dependable seed. But, like the genetically modified seed that would follow in its wake, it had one great advantage to the seed merchant and one disadvantage to the gardener: it did not set true seed. The gardener was obliged to return to their seed supplier year after year.

And it is the gardener's little winter bible, the seed catalogue, that reveals how times have changed in the seed industry. One British seed catalogue offered a selection of vegetables suitable for 'cold and temperate climates' in 1885. The list offered

 Bill Laws

58 beets, 145 cabbages, 74 onions and no less than 170 different peas. A century later a similar British seed catalogue could offer only six beetroot, 20 cabbages, five onions and ten varieties of peas.

30. Carl Linnaeus and the Classification of Vegetables

'Jan: 20. Hot-bed works very well. Hard frost for two or three days: now ground covered with snow. One of the hyacinths in the glafses seems to promise to blow soon.

'22. On this day, which was very bright, the sun shone very warm on the Hot-bed from a quarter before nine to three quarters after two. Very hard frost.

'29. On this day the mercury in the weather-glafses, which had been mounting leisurely for many days, was got one full degree above settled fair in the parlour, & within half a degree of the same in the study.'

The Reverend Gilbert White's *Garden Kalendar* for 1758 reflects the winter preoccupation of every vegetable gardener: the cold. In 1758 gardeners across the northern world watched the mercury fall at night and rise by day. Then, as now, they measured the temperature against the Celsius scale devised by Anders Celsius. For reasons best known to himself, however, Anders calibrated his scale so that nought represented the boiling point of water and 100 degrees its freezing point. Today we would be complaining still of a mild frost of 103 degrees had it not been for a chance meeting between Anders' uncle, the genial Olaf Rudbeck, and an impoverished Swedish student, Carl Linnaeus, at Uppsala in 1729. Rudbeck took the 22-year-old in and fed him. Linnaeus would later persuade Olaf's nephew Anders to reverse his calibration.

Linnaeus not only set the standard calibration for the kitchen garden thermometer, he also learned how to grow bananas successfully in the Netherlands and set the standards for many of the modern botanical gardens from the National Botanical Garden of Wales to Ogród Botaniczny in Warsaw.

But his most important contribution to the vegetable world was to devise a system of classifying vegetables and every other living form. While one colleague described his work as 'lewd and licentious,' Linnaeus had the satisfaction of having his system of classification adopted around the globe. We use it still today.

Carl Linnaeus was born in a simple turf-roofed timber cabin at Råshult near the shores of Lake Mökeln in the southern province of Sweden on May 23 1707, the oldest child of Nils Ingemarsson Linnaeus. Nils had adopted the name Linnaeus when he attended the university at Uppsala, taking the title from a favourite tree that had grown at a former family home. The tree was a lime or linden; forty years later it would become *Tilia cordata,* thanks to Linnaeus.

Nils was the parish priest and a fanciful gardener. He once created a curious raised bed to represent the family dining table with shrubs to portray the dinner guests sitting down to a meal. Carl was as intrigued by this horticultural oddity as he was by the natural world in general. Even at five, out walking with his father Carl would quiz Nils on the local names of plants. Nils is said to have reprimanded the boy and told him to commit the correct names to memory.

He also gave the child a plot of his own to cultivate. The garden is a good educator and Carl, like his younger brother Samuel, became a committed naturalist and gardener. This passion for gardening had unfortunate consequences for Samuel Linnaeus. Some years later when Carl failed to follow his father into the priesthood, his tutor told his parents that the young man's academic shortcomings were entirely due to his horticultural obsession. Fearing that Samuel would prove a second disappointment, Linnaeus' mother banned Samuel from meddling with plants. (The boy turned his attention to bees instead, a subject on which he would become a world authority.)

Carl went to study medicine rather than theology at his father's old university in Uppsala. Here he became friends with Peter Artedi, a fellow student who shared his fascination for the natural world. The two young men hatched an ambitious plan: together they would classify all of God's plants and creatures in a systematic fashion.

Until then every vegetable and plant had a variety of local or vernacular names and several, sometimes conflicting, Latin names. A Greek physician, Pedanius Dioscorides, had diligently named over 500 plants in his *De Materia Medica* around the time of Christ, but it took almost a thousand years before his work was disseminated first through the Arabic and then the Latin world.

Linnaeus and Artedi divided the task of classifying the animal and plant kingdoms between them and swore that whomever finished first would then come to the aid of his friend. But in 1735 Artedi died after falling into an Amsterdam canal and drowning. Linnaeus took on all the work himself. By the time he died in 1778, (some say of over work) Linnaeus had introduced a system for naming vegetables - and every other plant - that endures to this day.

Botanists and naturalists were agreed that plants fell into families. Onions, leeks, and garlic, for example, belonged to the allium family; beans and peas to the legume family; cabbages and cauliflowers to the brassica family; sweet corn to the grass family. What Linnaeus did was to introduce a two-word name for every plant within the families.

Plant families could be subdivided into distinct groups (or genera) and Linnaeus used the genus for the first name: *Pastinaca* from the Latin *pascare* (to feed) for the parsnip, for example, and *Pisum* for the pea.

Each group or genus could be divided again, this time into species. Linnaeus used his second Latin name to denote the species so the garden pea became *Pisum sativa* as distinct from the Mediterranean pea, *Pisum elatium*. Finally, each species could be further divided to include cultivated varieties or cultivars. As well as inventing a standard use of Latin words for every plant, Linnaeus also provided an international starting point for the old botanical names when he published his *Species Plantarum* in 1753.

Linnaeus classified the genus and species of plants according to the number of stamens and stigmas, a 'sexual system' of classification. One of his friends was John Siegesbeck, a St Petersburg academic after whom Linnaeus named the Sigesbeckia. But the two fell out when Siegesbeck denounced his former friend's work as 'lewd'. How, he ranted, could onions be up to such vegetative immorality? What was worse: how could young people be taught 'so licentious a method' of classification? Despite the 'loathsome harlotry' of his system, it was adopted universally and Linnaeus became a household name.

Linnaeus also showed the kitchen gardener that the successful cultivation of any vegetable depended on duplicating as closely as possible the plant's natural origins, soil and climate. (He would later advise the curators of botanical gardens to keep separate hot, warm and cold glasshouses as well as an outdoor area so that they might replicate local growing conditions, which laid the foundations for contemporary dome gardens such as the Eden project.)

In spite of his celebrity status, Linnaeus was a modest man. For his funeral arrangements he stipulated: 'Entertain nobody at my funeral, and accept no condolences.' But when he died on January 22 1778, his instructions were ignored. A stately funeral was held at Uppsala Cathedral and even the King of Sweden came to pay his respects to the man who gave a name to every vegetable in the world.

Book IV - Vegetable Bounty

31. Vegetable Healing

If the biblical Garden of Eden, with its temptingly forbidden fruit, was a place of paradise, the down-to-earth kitchen garden was a place of healing. John Gerard, for example, thought the lettuce 'cooleth the heat of the stomacke, called the heart-burning; and helpeth it when it is troubled with choler; it quencheth thirst, and causeth sleepe.'

The fruit of the cucmber, meanwhile, 'cut in pieces or chopped as herbes to the pot' and taken three times a day 'doth perfectly cure all manner of sauce flegme and copper faces, red and shining fieries noses ... and such like precious faces.'

Much of the information about the vegetable herbal reached Europe from Africa and the Middle East. Following their invasion of Persia in the 7th century, Arab conquerors absorbed rather than destroyed the civilised Persian gardens, which were stocked with useful plants. The Moors carried this horticultural knowledge and their pharmaceutical texts with them as they moved up through Spain in the 800s and introduced their own citrus fruits and 'new' vegetables such as cauliflowers, red-rooted carrots, cardoons, aubergines and artichokes. Artichokes were a celebrated aphrodisiac, but the aubergine had mysterious properties: while Moors could consume them with impunity, it was said that Christians risked death if they ate them.

This sometimes suspect knowledge was carried up through Europe, especially in the royal courts: kings and queens naturally expected to benefit from the very latest medical opinion. Scholars, too, passed on the plant pharmacology from monastery to monastery. Here in the medieval hierarchy God was the chief physician although the monk might do what he could to alleviate suffering. The Infirmarer (the term infirmary, carried to the New World by the founding fathers, outlived its use in Europe) expected his gardeners in the infirmary garden to be able to identify, cultivate and prepare medicinal concoctions for his patients and convalescing monks. Stress is nothing new; bled six times a year to alleviate anxiety, the monks would afterwards receive nourishing vegetables from the abbey gardens and be allowed the quiet stimulation of conversation in the pleasant surroundings of the parlour (from *parler* to talk). On the subject of bleeding, a male horror of menstruation led some to advocate that a woman 'in her terms' should not enter the melonry for fear that the fruit would drop off. Early authorities declared that if a young woman, menstruating for the first time, was led around the cabbage patch it would kill any caterpillars on the crop. But the gardener had to take care: young plants would die if a woman in menstruation so much as looked at them.

The monastic arsenal of medicinal plants included herbs, spices and vegetables. No distinction was made between vegetables and other medicinal plants until the mid 1700s - everything that grew in the kitchen garden was thought to have healthy properties. The apothecary advocated diets of salads and healing vegetables for the 'pottage' while the yeoman and his wife

Fifty Tales from the Kitchen Garden

grew a steady supply of herbal plants and vegetables in the garden - there is nothing new about the idea of a healthy diet.

From the Middle Ages to the late 1800s physicians took a holistic approach to their patients' ills, advocating good air, exercise, rest and, on the premise that a little of what you fancy does you good, a modicum of strong emotions such as pleasure or anxiety. A mother, meanwhile, relied on her hand-me-down down knowledge and experience to care for a sick child or relative. She would be familiar with hedgerow cures, treating worms with vermicidal plants such as mugwort or wormwood, for example, or prescribing salads, pottages and tisanes (an infusion of dried herbs) for a particular condition. Until the 1400s, however, she could only update that knowledge from hearsay since her gender kept her in a state of illiteracy, particularly of the *lingua medicina*, the language of medicine, Latin. Gradually these Latin texts were translated and pirated copies of the books were circulated around the country homes.

So it was she learned that the wild parsnip in a decoction helped the bowels to move and the urine to flow while oil extracted from the seeds could soothe intermittent fevers such as malaria. From Thomas Hill's Gardeners Labyrinth of 1577 she discovered even greater benefits: 'Parsnep removeth the venereal act, procureth Urine, and asswageth the Cholerick, sendeth down the Termes in Women; it profiteth the Melanchollicke, encreaseth good blood, helpeth the straightnese of making water, amendeth stitches of the sides or purisies, the bite of venemous beast, it amendeth the eating of Ulcers, the wearing of this root is profitable.' You might feel foolish pinning your *parsnep* to your cloak, but at least you knew it was doing you good.

The leek featured as a cure for an inflammation of the arm when it was used as a hot poultice. If the housewife could plan ahead she might take advantage of the knowledge that celery boiled with oil and sweet beer and swallowed four days in a row acted as a contraceptive. It would treat blood-shot eyes if mixed with resinous frankincense and, mixed with any oil, was a salve for sore joints. Wild celery was a laxative and diuretic, relieving swellings and breaking up gallstones. For the prevention of kidney stones, seakale was the answer, according to the apothecary William Curtis in 1799. The up and coming potato had its uses too. Early potatoes fetched a high price as an aphrodisiac while a potato was a sure charm against rheumatism - but only if it had been stolen. A slice of potato rubbed over a wart and then buried, caused the wart to disappear.

Garlic was used as an antiseptic even during the First World War while the onion was a prophetic vegetable: the thickening of onion skins were sure signs of a bad winter approaching.

Leaf crops were always useful. Parsley was a cure for stomach ache, as Beatrix Potter noted in *The Tale of Peter Rabbit*: '[Peter] ate some radishes; and then, feeling rather sick, he went to look for some parsley'. Less well known, except to the Romans, was the idea that parsley could cure sick fish if scattered on the surface of the pond.

Since lettuce, the sacred plant of the Egyptian goddess of fertility, was used in sacrifices, it was forbidden food for the temple priests. For the laity, however, it made a healing poultice and could cure stomach aches and coughs. While Greeks and Romans ate their lettuces last thing at night to calm the mind and induce sleep, the lettuce also promised to cleanse the blood, promote milk in nursing mothers, cure excessive drinking and counter impotence. (The Romans believed that eating raw, pickled cabbage before a meal countered the effects of alcohol)

The bean was another life saver. Henry Thoreau noted a Roman passion for beans 'not that I wanted beans to eat, for I am by nature a Pythagorean, so far as beans are concerned,

Fifty Tales from the Kitchen Garden

whether they mean porridge or voting,' he explained in 1845. (The Greek Pythagoreans, believing that the soul passed on into another body after death, had an aversion to the foetal-shaped beans which seemed to presage the germ of life, while it was a custom of Roman politicians to distributed free beans to bolster their chances at the polls.) The Celts supposedly celebrated with a bean feast, Scottish witches reputedly rode not broomsticks, but bean-stalks, and it was expedient to carry a bean or two with you on dark nights: ghosts were sent packing if you spat a bean at them. Gerard noted that the pea was 'not so windy as be the beans,' but there were fraudulent overtones to giving a man 'a pea for a bean'. Religious customs had plenty of uses for the vegetable crop. Onions, leeks and colewort were dutifully eaten during Lent while carlin peas, grown in the north-east of England, were soaked overnight and eaten on Passion or Carlin Sunday. Whether this was a religious rite or a stop gap meal at a time of year when the vegetable plot was depleted is not recorded.

Although Pliny the Elder had recorded no less than 87 cabbage-related medicines, the general view of vegetables through the 1700s and 1800s was that, while they might cure you of one or two ailments, they were basically not to be trusted. In the Elizabethan age, for example, the potentially healthy benefits of vegetables were lost on the sailing fraternity who rarely listed fresh vegetables among their ships' provisions. On board, a diet of dried beans was bad enough without adding beetroot, which was said to cause flatulence. Dysentery and malaria were said to be symptoms, not of contaminated water or mosquitoes, but the wholly innocent cucumber. Nicholas Culpeper, meanwhile, had already condemned that other salad crop, the radish, in his *Compleat Herbal*: 'Garden radishes are in wantonness by the gentry eaten as a salad, but they breed but scurvy humours in

 Bill Laws

the stomach, and corrupt the blood, and then send for a physician as fast as you can,' he advised.

Not until the 1800s did the Admiralty accept the necessity of dosing its sailors with lemon juice to counter scurvy. In the interests of economy, however, they carried the cheaper, and less effective, limes from the British colonies; ever after the Americans referred to the British sailors as limeys. But by the mid 1800s attitudes to vegetables were changing on both sides of the Atlantic. 'The garden pays full as well as the field,' advised one North American farmer in a periodical of 1859. Twenty years on a Mr Hood was corresponding with the *Canadian Horticulturalist* on the healthy benefits of eating tomatoes and increasing 'one's hopes of longevity. How glorious a thing to be able, like Macbeth, to say "Throw physic to the dogs", and rejoice in the diminution of your doctor's bills.'

In Europe during this period the householder was more concerned with taste than the supposedly healthy benefits of the vegetable although it was soon apparent that those forced to live in the city slums were dying on their impoverished diets. In 1899 when the British nation needed healthy recruits to fight the Boers, they found the average farm hand fit enough, but 90 per cent of one contingent of over one thousand volunteers from the city of Manchester were rejected on the grounds of ill health.

It took two World Wars to drive home the message that greens were good for you. 'Gardens are still in the news,' wrote a Toronto columnist Collier Stevenson in 1943, for 'the raising of vitamin- and mineral-rich vegetables, both for the nutritional and economic advantage to Canada.'

In North America the horticultural debate was less concerned with the healthy benefits or otherwise of the vegetable, but over where the kitchen gardener stood: were they for organic gardening? Or chemicals? The dust bowl disaster of 1935 when

Fifty Tales from the Kitchen Garden

tons of topsoil were blown off the heavily fertilised fields of the American west ruined farmers and triggered the beginnings of a crisis of confidence between the consumer and the chemical fertiliser industry. The campaigns of New Yorker Jerome I Rodale (the *New York Times* called him the 'Guru of the Organic Food Cult') and his *Organic Gardening* magazine, Rachel Carson's *Silent Spring*, and growing concerns over sources of environmental pollution from nuclear fallout to farm pesticides moved the argument along in favour of the organic gardener. It boosted the arrival of a new kind of store designed to cater specifically for those who were worried about their health, the wholefood and health food store.

In the UK, when a free health service was being offered to the nation in the aftermath of the Second World War, western medicine placed its faith firmly in pharmaceuticals and surgery. The herbalists, who, before the war, had traded on every high street in the country, packed up their plants and potions, went away, taking with them twenty centuries of wisdom. Yet, while 25% of the world's medicines were based on plant extracts, only an estimated ten per cent of the world's species of plants had been properly analysed.

Gradually vegetable remedies made a comeback, filling the shelves of the new breed of health stores which had crossed over from the America. When, in 2003, Dr John Briffa was telling the readers of his column in the *Observer* magazine that 'the onion packs an eye-watering nutritional punch' he was only repeating the views of ancient Indian, Egyptian, Chinese and Roman physicians centuries before.

32. Popeye The Spinach Man

One vegetable whose healthy benefits were unknown to the Greek and Roman medics was spinach. It arrived from Persia in the 6th century, but the American Elzie Segar had no doubts about its healthy properties when he began sketching out a cartoon character to woo Castor Oyl. This was the muscle-bound hero, Popeye The Sailor Man, who was 'strong to the finich, 'cos I eat me spinach'.

Spinach (we now know) is rich in lutein and zeaxanthin which, like the more familiar betacarotene, are antioxidants that help to combat free radicals, the molecules that are especially damaging to the proteins in the lens of the human eye and contribute to eye cataracts. Popeye, with his fine eyesight was appropriately, if inadvertently, named.

33. The Vegetarian Movement

'We must cultivate our garden,' Voltaire declared in his *Candide*, published in 1759. He had a special interest in the contents of the vegetable patch since he and others including the poets Alexander Pope and Percy Bysshe Shelley and the pastor John Wesley, promoted the virtues of a meat-free diet. No one took them very seriously until 1847 when a group of Christians and physicians met up at a hospital in Ramsgate, Kent to form the Vegetarian Society. The group included the Horsells who ran the hospital on vegetarian lines, the Member of Parliament for Salford, Joseph Brotherton, and his wife Martha and they took their name from the same Latin root as the vegetable: vegere, to enliven and to animate.

Later that year the Manchester branch of the Society was launched with a celebratory meal of onion and sage fritters, savoury pie and plum pudding. The recipes were based on Britain's first non-flesh cookery book, which had been published in 1821 by Martha Brotherton after her encounter with the oddly named Reverend William Cowherd.

 Bill Laws

The Salford clergyman abhorred the eating of flesh. He took to the streets to run a soup kitchen, distributing free vegetable soup to the poor and earnestly preaching a 'live and let live' message to the congregation at his Bible Christian Church. At a time when meat was expensive and food scares common, he gained a significant following.

A party of converts from the Church migrated to Philadelphia in 1817 with Reverend William Metcalfe and his wife Suzanne. Pious if unpopular, Metcalfe eventually met with Amos Bronson Alcott, father of Louisa May Alcott the author of Little Women, and neighbour of Henry Thoreau, and a biscuit manufacturer Sylvester Graham (who espoused a diet of raw food only) to found the American Vegetarian Society in 1850. The movement attracted many 19th century celebrities including Annie Besant (who founded the influential Theosophical Society), the shorthand inventor Isaac Pitman, the Russian novelist Leo Tolstoy, Mahatma Gandhi and novelist and playwright George Bernard Shaw. The Vegetarians, however, were not so much pro-vegetable eaters as anti-meat. 'Animals are my friends and I don't eat my friends,' explained Shaw.

34. To Market

Every spring avalanches of green artichokes and asparagus cascade across the marble counters of the *Modernismo* market hall in Valencia. In Amsterdam's Boerenmarkt, red, green and yellow tomatoes, peppers and aubergines are arranged in Rastafarian-coloured patterns. Fat, ripe pumpkins surround farm pick-ups at a Kingston, Canada country market in the Fall.

Fresh vegetables always make a pretty picture, but nothing quite matches the French village market. This is a nation that knows its onions. From the summer run of Citroen vans laden with tomatoes, early potatoes and *haricot vert* in le Midi to the autumn harvest of the Basque pimento, sold to be hung out to dry on the half timbered house fronts, the French are past masters at bringing their vegetables fresh to market.

The freshest vegetables are those with the shortest journey between kitchen garden and kitchen table, the home-grown variety. Most households, however, learned to rely on markets and shops for their fresh veg. Some of the produce was well travelled. In the UK leeks, deflagged (with their tops cut) so they could fit their plastic containers, would be trucked across country from the fields of Lincolnshire to a packing and distribution centre in south-east England before being driven back to the Lincolnshire supermarkets for sale. In 2013 figures from the European Union showed that over 50% of vegetables from the Union's three main producers, Romania, Poland and Lithuania, were still moved by road. It left the price of vegetables inextricably linked to the cost of truck fuel.

Northern Europe had also grown accustomed to receiving bunches of beans, ruler-straight and measuring no more than 3.7 inches (9.5 cm) so as to snugly fit their cling-filmed plastic trays, arriving by air from Kenya. Christmas peas and Easter carrots winged their way to Ireland from South Africa, a journey of nearly 6,000 miles, while sugar snap peas arrived, out-of-season in Sweden, from Guatemala. Cheap labour led to some extravagant vegetable journeys: one supermarket chain used to retail attractive trays of miniature vegetables tied with a blade of chives. But before they reached the chilled supermarket shelf, packaging and chives were first flown out of the UK to Kenya's Nairobi airport. Here local women tied the green blades of chives around a selection of Kenyan-grown vegetables before the finished packages were returned by air to the UK.

Air miles, road miles and excessive packaging of what are essentially already-packed (in their skins) vegetables led to environmental protests. The cost of this global vegetable market, it was claimed, was over reliant on non-renewable resources, given the growing concerns over global warming and climate change. There were consumer boycotts and campaigns to persuade more people to 'eat local'. But others pointed out that many of these 'third world' crops were grown and harvested with non-intensive manual labour using low-tech irrigation systems and natural fertilisers (cow manure) compared to the fossil-fuel hungry methods employed at home.

Fifty Tales from the Kitchen Garden

The new global vegetable market attracted other criticisms. By the late 1900s, as the US started to sell the first genetically modified tomato (its inactive ripening gene left it looking fit and well long after it had been harvested), restaurateurs and cooks complained that vegetables were being selected for their convenient shape and size rather than for their taste.

Supermarkets countered that the neatly packaged, seasonless vegetable was the natural consequence of consumer choice. The rise of the supermarket to supremacy in the vegetable market place seemed to support their claims: in the 1970s, wholesalers marketed 90% of vegetables and fruit in Britain. Thirty years later the supermarkets had taken over 80% of the market share. And their share was growing.

Supermarkets had started off quietly enough. In 1869 John Sainsbury and his wife established a shop in Drury Lane, just down the road from the Covent Garden market in London. One hundred and thirty years later his business had become the third largest supermarket chain in the UK. In the early 1900s Jack Cohen, a young barrow boy, was working in the London markets. He turned a small profit selling surplus army rations and then in 1924 bought a supply of tea from one T.E. Stockwell, sold it again at a profit and founded a small company using the initial letters of his tea supplier with his own surname to create Tesco. A visit to America convinced him that the self-service store was a thing of the future and that extending his lines to include non-food stuffs would create a kind of 'super market'.

As the new generation of Sainsburys and Cohens firmed up their global networks of fresh vegetables, the trend was clear: the high street greengrocers and the neighbourhood shop were in free fall. Their numbers, 113,000 in 2003, had dropped by almost 20% in ten years: during the same decade the floor space of the major supermarkets had increased by 50%. Fruit and vegetables were a profitable trade and one worth competing for. With an average mark up of 40% on fruit and vegetables, the produce aisle of the supermarket was now one of the most lucrative parts of the store.

35. Traditional Traders

Supermarkets have proved to be successful hucksters in edging out their rivals, yet there is nothing novel about competitive practises in the vegetable market. During the reign of Elizabeth 1, for example, housewives were being persuaded to buy new, improved peas, sold green rather than dreary dry for winter storage. Long journey times for vegetables were nothing new either. The Emperor Tiberius was said to have had his parsnips imported to Rome from the banks of the Rhine in Germany. And before it was removed because of the 'scurrility, clamour and nuisance of the gardeners and their servants,' the 14th century market near London's St Paul's, where the 'gardeners of earls, barons, bishops and citizens sold their produce,' was provisioned by foot, sail power and the plodding pack horse. The ridgeways, drove roads and salt ways of England carried a steady traffic of cabbage-mongers, garlic-mongers and leek-mongers heading for market with baskets and trays of vegetables for sale.

During the hungry gap between the end of winter and the harvesting of their first vegetables, the poor were entitled by law to pick green peas in the field for their own consumption:

hucksters were regularly reprimanded for trying to sell their pickings at market. A more reliable supplier was the local monastery garden, until Henry VIII sequestered the wealth of the monasteries and redistributed it amongst his friends. The Cistercian order, founded in 1098 in Burgundy, France, advocated self sufficiency in the garden and invested time and effort in good tools and efficient growing methods. The cellarer at Westminster's convent garden, for example, had to supply the monastery with fresh vegetables and herbs, hay for the floors and the *garderobes*, and rushes, mints and meadowsweet for strewing across the floorboards. He had to look after his hedged plots, his house cows and their pasture, and his hives of bees for the honey and wax. There was always surplus produce to be sold at market or traded for seed and cuttings.

The vegetable gardens of earls, barons and bishops also played their part. Head gardeners were often expected to supplement their income from the sale of surplus produce. At Stow Bardolph in Norfolk a contract for the head gardener of 1712 stipulated that he 'maintain and keep and furnish ... Stow Hall ... with all necessary and sufficient kitchen garden stuffe'. It also allowed him to pocket the profits from the sale of vegetables to top up his wage of £50 a year.

Vegetables were traded from country to country too. Vegetables had been shipped from France and the Low Countries across to England as early as the 1300s. One of the popular destinations was the old Westminster convent garden, later the Covent Garden and one of several markets claiming the title of London's Larder. Inland journey times between the market garden and the market were driven down as roads, carts and carriages improved. They improved even more when, in the 1820s, three thousand miles of new canal were added to Britain's transport network. Like France's Canal du Midi (1681),

Fifty Tales from the Kitchen Garden

New York's Erie Canal (1825) and Germany's Eiderkanal, these waterways also improved the fertility of neighbouring fields and gardens: 'Fields, which before were barren, are now drained, and by the assistance of manure, conveyed on the canal toll-free, are clothed with a beautiful verdure,' noted Thomas Pennant in 1782 when he surveyed the landscape around the new Grand Junction Canal between Trent and Mersey.

Soon streaming along behind were the world's railways. By the 1850s a Scottish laird wintering in the south for the London season, could, and did, expect the produce of his walled kitchen garden outside Edinburgh to be picked, packed and put on the train to London 350 miles (563 kilometres) away so that it might arrive on the doorstep of his Chelsea villa in a matter of hours. The transport of vegetables - and everything else - had been revolutionised.

'Crowds of people and mountains of goods, departing and arriving scores upon scores of times in every four-and-twenty hours, produced a fermentation in the place that was always in action,' observed the Victorian author Charles Dickens (1812–1870) in *Dombey and Sons* as he watched London's Camden Town railway develop in 1836. 'There were railway patterns in its drapers' shops, and railway journals in the windows of its newsmen. There were railway hotels, office-houses, lodging-houses, boarding-houses; railway plans, maps, views, wrappers, bottles, sandwich-boxes, and time-tables.' The 'dunghills, dustheaps, and ditches and gardens, and summerhouses' of the area, meanwhile, had disappeared as families moved out of town, along the lifeline of the railway, to settle in the country and grow their vegetables there.

Not that the railways were welcomed with open arms. Some were as bitterly opposed to them as their descendants would be to the motorways of the 21st century. 'We are too much hurrying about in these islands; much for idle pleasure, and more from over activity in the pursuit of wealth, without regard to the good or happiness of others,' mourned the poet William Wordsworth when plans were announced for a line from Kendal to his favourite Lake Windermere.

What was done was not to be undone. Townships lobbied for the railways to pass on their doorsteps while manufacturers emphasised their proximity to the railways: 'The facilities we have on all hands - sea, canal, and rail - for despatching Manures of our usual high standard ... enable us to ensure the prompt delivery of all orders with which we may be favoured,' promised the seeds company, Webbs of Stourbridge. Markets adjusted their working hours to coincide with the train deliveries and, for a century, railway traffic reigned supreme as small agricultural armies of pickers were formed in the shires to gather the vegetables fresh and send them by the wagon and cart load to the station. Itinerant pickers followed the ripening crops from region to region, swelling the ranks of the local seasonal pickers, mostly women and young children.

This Shropshire man recalled how his summer holidays were spent gathering fruit and vegetables in the 1930s. 'You used to be off school for four weeks picking to buy shoes and clothes to go back to school because your parents couldn't afford them. The produce used to be put in baskets and sent at night on the mail train to Birmingham, to the market there.' Twenty years later ex-soldiers found themselves picking vegetables in post war Britain: 'In the army we'd dreamed of returning to "blighty" and perhaps running a little country pub somewhere. Instead I found myself picking Brussel sprouts for the London train, in driving snow up on the cliff top above West Runton and crying with the cold.' Improvements in the weather were not matched by improvements in conditions: 'It was all hand work and in all weathers. We had a horse drawn hoe for the currant crop, but carrots and turnips were hoed out by hand, and beet was topped and tailed with a sickle.' Fifty years on and pickers were sending the produce direct to vast distribution centres from where they were trucked and flown to their final destination – the shopper's trolley.

But this world-wide market, created to fill the shelves as profitably as possible, had its critics. One was the Indian activist, Vandana Shiva who claimed that a global monoculture was being forced on people 'by defining everything that is fresh, local and handmade as a health hazard. Human hands are being defined as the worst contaminants, and work for human hands is being outlawed, to be replaced by machines and chemicals bought from global corporations.'

Supporters of her views, insisting that quality was being sacrificed for quantity, spurned the supermarkets and patronised farm shops, local markets and vegetable box schemes where householders bought only locally available vegetables that were in season. They seemed, for the time being at least, unlikely rivals to the might of the supermarket.

36. London's Larder

Covent Garden was the once largest fruit and vegetable market in the UK. Until the 1600s, grain grew in the fields and vegetables in the gardens that surrounded the convent of St Peter of Westminster. The convent had been built on an old Saxon site, part of a 9th century settlement called Lundenwic and one which was regularly threatened by Viking invaders sailing up river to plunder the town. The convent grounds declined after the dissolution of the monasteries by Henry VIII in the 1500s, until a London developer, the Earl of Bedford, proposed an radical experiment in town planning. With the enthusiastic support of King Charles 1, the Earl persuaded the most important architect of his day, Inigo Jones, to design a classical public square. Drawing on his experience of the classical Italian *piazza*, Jones demolished the winding alleys and lanes of the immediate neighbourhood and introduced the formal square to the people of London. As the convent gardens were buried beneath the foundations of the smart new town houses and Jones' classical church of Saint Paul, the public spilled into the square to admire his work. Unfortunately for the Earl of Bedford, the public nature of the square was its undoing and the wealthy, having so recently moved in, were soon moving out again to more private, neighbouring squares.

As the rich departed out, the fruit and vegetables moved in. A small market had stood here in 1649 surrounded by bordellos, coffee shops and Turkish bathing houses. It expanded gradually until, by the 1830s, it could rightfully claim to be the larder of London. At its height Covent Garden employed over a thousand porters and barrow boys. 'The wall-like regularity with which cabbage, cauliflowers, and turnips are built up to a height of some twelve feet is nothing short of marvellous,' reported an enthusiastic Charles Dickens. In 1886 Covent Garden Market opened a new floral hall and market gardeners and country house head gardeners alike fed the market their produce.

In 1974 the old Garden was finally closed and a new one opened at Nine Elms in Vauxhall. After a battle by conservationists over plans to redevelop the Garden, campaigners won the day, the Secretary of State promised to preserve the main buildings and the Garden was turned into the tourist market it is today.

37. Onion Johnnies

It was an inadvertent, but briefly successful marketing ploy by Breton onion growers which led to the French stereotype of a *garçon* in a striped vest, sailor's trousers and black beret precariously riding a bicycle with a *baton* of bread or a string of onions across the handlebars.

Times were hard in Brittany *l'entre-deux-guerres,* between the two World Wars, and nowhere more so than on the north coast of Brittany in the onion growing region around Trégor. Here the young men wore the Breton beret, and the sailors their striped shirts just as their fathers and grandfathers had before them. But unlike their forefathers the young men were ready to travel and earn some money. In late summer when the onion crops were gathered in at villages like Yffiniac, near St Brieuc the young men would borrow the family bike and, carrying as many strings of onions as they could across the handlebars, ride down to the fishing ports of Saint-Brieuc or Tréguier to hitch a ride to the English ports. The traditional *journee d'Albion,* or the journey to Albion, brought early onions to the English south coast in what was mistakenly assumed by the cartoonists of the day to be the traditional French costume.

In 2003 the Breton town of Roscoff announced the opening of a museum dedicated to the 'Johnny Onion' as their door-to-door onion salesmen were known.

38. Vegetables Preserved

In the early 1800s the French navy, under blockade from the British, set sail from the port of Brest with a secret weapon on board. Hidden below decks were rows of champagne bottles filled, not with fine wine from that region, but beans, peas and boiled beef in gravy. The bottles were kept sealed for three months before they were opened and their contents sampled. While the beef tea was judged rather weak, the beans and peas were considered to have all the freshness and flavour of new picked vegetables - high praise from a nation that traditionally cast a hyper-critical eye on the quality of their vegetables.

The bottles had been prepared by Nicholas Appert, the chef and confectioner who invented the process of canning vegetables, fruit and meat. Born at Chalôns-sur-Marne on the edge of the Champagne region in 1750 where his father worked as a brewer and innkeeper, Appert died in 1841, his culinary contribution all but forgotten. Not until a French postage stamp was issued in his honour in 1955 was Monsieur Appert's genius acknowledged.

Appert had moved to Paris in 1781 and began experimenting with preserving food, filling his champagne bottles with different vegetables, fruit and meat and standing them in hot water before sealing them. After the success of the naval sea trials Appert, now living at Masy near Paris, set up the world's first canning factory - except that he was still using bottles, specially made to his design and stored in canvas bags to protect his workers from flying glass, should a bottle explode. His little factory was filled with cauldrons and copper boilers, kitchens and cold stores, bottle racks and cork stoppers, all devoted to storing and preserving food in such a way that the consumer could enjoy 'the month of May in the heart of winter' as his patron Grimond de La Reynière put it.

The business went well: forty women worked in the factory during the busy vegetable harvest and Appert's preserves sold in the Paris shops. The commercial potential of Appert's invention began to dawn on French government officials: preserved French vegetables could be sold for export; naval vessels could stay at sea for longer periods; and less food would need to be preserved by the traditional way, in sugar. (A sea blockade by the British had put sugar in short supply.) Appert, always generous with his research, was commissioned by the government to reveal the secrets of his process. But just as his book, *L'Art de Conserver Pendant Plusiers Années Toutes les Substances Animales et Végetales,* appeared in 1810 a Londoner, Peter Durand, patented the process and a London engineering company began preserving food by Appert's methods, using cans rather than bottles. Appert's own business floundered until, in the 1830s, he found the finance to set up another factory to bottle and can vegetables. By now the competition was too intense. The business failed and poor Appert died in obscurity and poverty.

Fifty Tales from the Kitchen Garden

The French may have forgotten Appert, but they did not forget his bottled vegetables, still a staple line in French food shops today. Shelves of bottled and canned vegetables, however, were about to make way for a new piece of equipment in the store, the freezer cabinet.

The post war vegetable, served in the 'meat and two veg' style, was a poor and watery thing. A 1950s author who offered sensible advice on travelling etiquette - 'if talking with strangers leads to further conversation, it should remain impersonal' - also offered useful advice on cooking vegetables: 'Vegetables: Boiling. All vegetables grown above ground should be boiled with the lid off the saucepan whilst those grown under should have the lid kept on.' She was not going to advocate the art of steaming vegetables or celebrating the vegetable in the French fashion where each course of vegetables was served and savoured separately. Clarence Birdseye's frosted vegetables were about to change all that.

What Eleanor Birdseye missed most about life as a fur trapper's wife in Labrador in the early years of the 1900s was fresh, green vegetables. She lived with her husband, Clarence or Bob as he preferred to be called, and their son Kellogg in a three roomed cabin 250 miles (402 kilometres) away from the nearest store or doctor. Bob, born in 1886 in New York, dropped out of Amherst College in Massachusetts because his family could not afford the fees. For a brief period he took a job with the US Department of Agriculture, but, always the risk taker, he persuaded Eleanor that there was a better living to be had from fur trapping. They moved to their lonely shack in north eastern Canada and they lived off home-frozen food.

Bob Birdseye learned quickly what the native north Canadians already knew, that meat tasted better if it was frozen fast. Fish, rabbit, duck and other game, naturally frozen outdoors in the

Arctic winds that drove temperatures down as low as -50 degrees centigrade kept its flavour. 'The Eskimos had used it for centuries. What I accomplished... was merely to make packaged frozen food available to the public,' he would say later.

To please Eleanor, Bob experimented with freezing vegetables. He stored cabbage brought by boat in barrels filled with salt water. 'Fresh' cabbage was then hacked out of the ice when required.

In 1917 the family returned to the United States and Bob Birdseye borrowed the corner of an ice cream factory in New Jersey where, in an effort to reproduce the Labrador winters by means of ice blocks, brine and an electric fan, he set up business selling frozen fish. The business went bust. The Birdseyes moved on, this time to the fishing port of Gloucester where the tenacious entrepreneur experimented with quick freezing meat, fish and vegetables. He built an automatic freezer that could fast freeze food when it was placed between metal plates that had been cooled to -40 degrees centigrade with calcium chloride brine. After patenting the process and setting up a new business, the General Seafoods Company, Bob Birdseye concentrated on improving his methods. Convinced of the need to freeze vegetables when they were still fresh he mobilised his quick freezer, mounting it on the back of a truck and driving it out into the fields where he could freeze the vegetables as they were picked. But business was slow and, at one point, he and Eleanor had to hock their insurance policies to keep it afloat. It was just as well since he would shortly receive what was then the largest single sum of money ever paid for a single process, 22 million dollars.

The pay-off came by chance. Marjorie Merryweather Post, the daughter of a food processing company owner, was taking a yachting holiday on the Massachusetts coast. One evening her chef served her roast goose bought in Gloucester from the

Fifty Tales from the Kitchen Garden

General Seafoods Company. When she learned that the fresh goose was actually several months old, she made an appointment to see Bob Birdseye. Three years later Bob's company was bought out by her family's firm and in 1930 the name changed to Birds Eye.

The millionaire Birdseyes settled into a new home where they could indulge their passion for horticulture. Bob was interested in hydroponics and believed there was enough growing space on the roofs and in the cellars of New York to feed the whole city with fresh vegetables by this method.

For the Birds Eye company, however, business was an uphill struggle. The frozen product might have revolutionised the processing of fresh vegetables, but storekeepers had to be persuaded to make room for a frozen food cabinet and housewives to add a freezer to their list of desirable white goods. Many housewives were reluctant not least because they were convinced that 'frosting' vegetables was merely a means of preserving second grade produce. But they had to concede that 'frosted peas' seemed to taste sweeter than fresh peas. It was true: frosted peas continued to convert starch into sugar even when frozen.

Birds Eye persisted, confident that a food revolution was on the way. Even in the 1930s they predicted that a day would come when the public would buy their food from a central store where butcher, delicatessen, greengrocer and fish shop were amalgamated. Who, asked the food writers, would welcome such a development? And why would anyone want to eat frozen peas at Christmas or 'fresh' fish, which was six months old? A glance into any supermarket trolley today tells its own story.

39. The Ice House

Freezing farm peas is a stop-watch affair where the grower has precisely 150 minutes to get the peas picked and chilled before they start to deteriorate. But long before Bob Birdseye patented his frosted food process, kitchen gardeners were rushing fresh vegetables to the ice house. Popularised by Charles II in England (he had an ice house built in St James Park in 1600), the ice house was all the rage among the country set of the 1700s and 1800s.

Built of stone or brick and set in the ground or the side of a hill, the pit of the house was filled with ice cut from some neighbouring lake during the winter. Packed down and kept dry, the ice would keep for twelve months or more. The chamber above the ice was lined with chilled shelves and rails where fresh vegetables and foods were stored until required. But, while the gardeners on estates like Dalmery Park, Dundas Castle and Doddington House were justly proud of their estate ice houses, ice had been used to chill food by the ancient Chinese and, remarkably, the Mesopotamian gardeners 4,000 years earlier. And Alexander the Great is said to have had trenches dug and filled with mountain snow and covered with branches at Petra so that his soldiers could still enjoy cool wine, fruit and vegetables even in the heat of summer.

40. A Vegetable Calendar

February
In the Saxon calendar, February was the month of the cabbage.

2. The first day to sow peas in England, but only if the weather was wet.

9. Birthday plant of the day is the leek. To eat leeks is to suffer humiliation.

17. Birthday plant is the pea, symbol of respect.

March
1. St David's Day when Welsh people traditionally wear the leek. St David instructed his brothers to wear a leek when they went in to battle against the Saxons.

1. An old country saying suggests this was the last day to sow peas.

Ash Wednesday - the traditional day to eat parsnips for those observing Lent.

Various. Lady day: traditionally the day to pay the allotment rent, or the start or end a farm tenancy.

 Bill Laws

April
Good Friday - the day to plant potatoes once they have been sprinkled with Holy Water.

May
National Asparagus Month

June
National Asparagus Festival, West Michigan.
13. Birthday plant of the day was the potato, the symbol of benevolence.
21. Time to lift your tree onion.
21. The last day for cutting asparagus in England.
21. The arrival of the first crop of peas, 'harbinger of summer,' according to Shirley Hibberd.

July
The World's biggest garlic festival at Gilroy, California.
26. St Anne's Day and Garlic and basil fair at Tours in France.

August
Annual Potato Festival at Alliston, the potato capital of Ontario.
Onion Festival, Roscoff, Brittany

September
Tomato Festival at Château de la Bourdaisière, Montlouis-sur-Loire, France.
Potimarron (a Japanese squash) Festival at Lunéville, France.
1. The Saint's Day of the spade.
19. Birthday plant is the cabbage, symbol of profit and gain.
27. Birthday plant is the dandelion, symbol of bitterness and grief.

Fifty Tales from the Kitchen Garden

October
Thanksgiving Day in Canada and pumpkin pie is on the menu.
 Halloween - scoop out a pumpkin and set a lighted candle inside.
 31. Birthday plant is the nettle, symbol of spite.

November
Annual display of unusual vegetables at Saint Jean de Beauregard, France
 Thanksgiving Day in the US - time for some pumpkin pie.

December
21. The young man who places an onion under his pillow will dream the face of his future wife.
 The shortest day - the time to plant the tree onion.
 22. According to the Roman, Columella, early cucumbers could be raised by cutting the down stem of a fennel or bramble and slotting the seed of a cucumber into the pith of the mother plant shortly after the winter equinox.

Book V – Vegetable Passions

41. Tildeling, kleingarten and ogród dzialkowy

America's wartime victory gardens gradually evolved into community gardens, neighbourhood projects that ranged from simple street planters offering passers by free, pickable food to ambitious gardening programmes that aimed to reconnect people with their food supplies. However the business of growing vegetables in allotments, garden colonies, chalet gardens or worker gardens dates back to the expansion of the cities in the late 1800s and early 1900s. As traditional back gardens were crowded out of town by the encroaching foundries, factories and mills, gardeners were forced to find land away from the home for their vegetables and flowers. In France the poor had to make do with a *lopin de terre*, a vegetable plot squeezed into some urban corner while the more fortunate found space for the *potager* on the *jardin ouvrier*, grouped together on the outskirts of town. The German equivalent was the *kleingarten* where rows of vegetables and flowers grew beside the barbecue, the habitable summerhouse and the social club. In Poland it was the *ogród dzialkowy*, a testament to *kombinować* (which might be loosely translated as making the best of very little), a model for similar garden allotments, which stretched across Europe from Helsinki to Helsingborg.

The sensible Danes were ahead of the horticultural game, claiming to have laid down the world's first allotments or *tildeling* under the towers and turrets of the fortified town of Fredericia back in 1778. The happy folk of Aalborg and Copenhagen had followed suit by the late 1800s, a horticultural initiative that was replicated across the Scandinavian world in Sweden, Norway and Finland.

The English word allotment originates from the Old French meaning to divide out and share, although in Britain its true roots lay in an act of land theft - the enclosures. In post medieval times most of Britain was still farmed on an open field system. By the 1500s, during the reign of Elizabeth 1, the process of parcelling up or enclosing the countryside had begun. Contrary to claims that enclosures were all for the greater good since they produced a more efficient agricultural system, enclosures robbed from the poor and gave to the already rich.

'Inclosure, thou'rt a curse upon the land,

And tasteless was the wretch who thy existence plann'd' declared John Clare, England's peasant poet, as he witnessed the rural poor grow poorer. Even some of those directly responsible for enclosures, like this secretary to one Agricultural Board, noted with concern that 'the poor are injured, in some, grossly injured.'

Early efforts to compensate the lower classes included the idea of 'alloting' small patches of waste land for the landless labourer to cultivate. Twenty-eight years after Fredericia's allotments were laid down, England's first enclosure allotments were provided at Great Somerford in Wiltshire when, as 970 acres

Fifty Tales from the Kitchen Garden

were enclosed, just under ten acres were set aside for allotments. As the legal Acts permitting enclosures were rushed through Parliament between 1760 and 1818, Members of Parliament were petitioned to include allotments in the legislation. Not until 1819, when the number of parish destitutes had increased so dramatically it threatened to overwhelm local communities, were parish wardens given legal powers to rent parcels of land, allotments, to its hungry villagers. It took another 26 years before every Act of Enclosure was legally required to provide the poor with a number of 'field gardens' each no bigger than a quarter of an acre.

Land owners who had, by now, gained more land and a workforce reliant on their largess, were troubled by the notion of allotments. They feared that labourers with allotments would steal their seeds. Worse still, the farmhands would slyly conserve their working energies during the day, only to expend them, selfishly, on their allotments at night. 'The extent of the garden of a labourer ought never to be such as to interfere with his employment as a labourer,' warned John Loudon. Parliament duly insisted that allotments should be small enough to prevent the labourer neglecting 'his usual paid labour'. Even this failed to satisfy the employers and many farmers refused employment to a worker who kept a parish allotment.

Such was the situation at Hitcham, Suffolk during the mid nineteenth century. Hitcham was a pretty place, its streets lined with half-timbered farmhouses, its church decorated with a fine 15th century hammerbeam roof. Hitcham, however, had a problem: a disproportionately high crime rate. Its rector in the 1840s was Reverend John Stevens Henslow (1796–1861), a good friend of the controversial evolutionist Charles Darwin, but a preacher with a poor reputation for sermonising. Henslow, nevertheless, was a minister with a mission for social reform and he established allotments on church land in an attempt to reduce local delinquency. The neighbouring farmers threatened to blacklist any labourer who dared rent one of his plots. The wise Mr Henslow responded by organising produce shows and vegetable competitions to which the great, the good and the poor cottager were all invited. Always a social leveller, these annual fruit and vegetable shows engendered a spirit of friendly rivalry and conciliation.

Benevolent industrialists followed Henslow's example. When the Yorkshire textile manufacturer Titus Salt built his new town on the banks of the river Aire outside Bradford (he proudly named it after himself: Saltaire), he provided 800 homes for his mill workers, each with a parlour, kitchen, pantry, three bedrooms, an outside lavatory and an allotment 'each not exceeding 15 poles in extent.' John Lawes, who patented the process for manufacturing artificial fertiliser not only established allotments for the workers on his Rothamsted Estate, but also provided a club house in which he expected his more temperant tenant gardeners to drink coffee in place of their customary beer. The expanding railway companies of the 19th century also provided allotments both for their own employees and the general public. The railway men would become one of the more generous suppliers of allotments, second only to local councils.

The National Agricultural Labourers Union, formed in 1870 and the farmers' foe for championing farm labourers' rights, actively campaigned for allotments for its members. But the government, more sympathetic to the landed gentry than to its farm hands, moved at a snail's pace. Eventually an Allotment Act was passed in 1887 after several allotment candidates had stood to challenge the sitting members of Parliament in a number of by-elections. One, a Liberal called Halley Stewart, won the Lincolnshire seat of Spalding in 1887 for the allotment

Fifty Tales from the Kitchen Garden

cause. When Stewart's victory failed to persuade parliament to stop prevaricating, allotment holders took their battle to the local elections and won such a round of victories that Parliament, fearing a rush of allotment MPs arriving at Westminster, finally admitted defeat. By 1895, at last, the number of allotments rose by 50% to 482,901.

Throughout the 1900s the allotment movement waxed and waned according to the economic tides: when jobs were plentiful, demand fell; when hard times hit, during the depression in the early 1930s, the oil crisis of the early 1970s and the global recession of the early 1990s, demand rose.

Back in 1918 when allotments were still classed as being 'for the labouring poor,' a National Union of Allotment Holders was founded in Britain. Four years earlier Denmark established its own Allotment Garden Union. In the 1980s the British Society had added the term 'Leisure Gardeners' to its title, a change of name that reflected a change of style in the allotments. Across Europe new people with new passions for vegetable growing were moving in and migrant workers from Asia, Africa and India introduced their own growing skills and vegetables to the allotments. Nottingham's Pat Garfoot and Henry Francis, originally from the West Indies and now a fellow allotment holder, were a case in point. The two men took on neighbouring allotments at Hunger Hill in Nottingham, but while Pat continued growing his traditional parsnips, spuds and cabbages - what his father had taught him to grow - Henry was planting pumpkin, beans and *calulu* (a type of West Indian spinach) just as his parents had in the West Indies. The two men began spicing up their fresh vegetables and hosting regular curry nights on the allotment. Such scenes had never been seen before.

In the States, too, a rich ethnic neighbourhood mix led to some cultural vegetable exchanges, especially after the launch of the Italian Carol Petrini's notions of slow food. Petrini had founded his food movement in 1986, an idea that was designed to celebrate local food and food production in a reaction against the rise of fast and fatty foods. Petrini, who was famously quoted as saying that a local cheese merited preserving just as much as a 16th century building, had been appalled by plans for a McDonald's burger joint in Rome. Now cities across the States were hosting their own food projects, which, although temporarily slowed by the economic recession of the early 2000s, were steadily spreading. Lauren Howe, a bright-eyed enthusiast and director of the National School Garden Program for Slow Food USA used street allotments gardening as a community building tool in Denver, Colorado: 'I believe in the power of gardens to educate people about where their food comes from, empower them to grow and cook their own food and reconnect them with nature.' Street gardens, she declared, had all the potential to become a focus for community life.

In the matter of urban planning however, allotments in the 21st century sometimes faced an uncertain future. Sometimes sited on potentially valuable land they often found themselves coming under the unwelcome gaze of property speculators.

In 2012 the Krakow Post reported on a legal threat to over one million allotments, 10,000 in Krakow alone. As the British TV gardener Monty Don told the *Observer* newspaper in 2015: 'Allotments are a paradigm of a successful society: we should treasure them.'

42. The Political Potato

'I do not hear that it hath been yet assayed whether they [potatoes] may not be propagated in great quantities, for food for swine or other cattle.' So wrote John Worlidge in his *Systema Agriculturae* in 1669. 'They are much used in Ireland and America as bread and may be propagated with advantage to poor people.'

Nowadays we all like our potatoes. People in Peru like them too: they have been eating them for 5,000 years. Four thousand-year-old shards of pottery from the region suggest they worshipped, or at least venerated, the crop as well. Since then the potato has become one of most important crops in the world after corn (maize), wheat and rice and is eaten by more people now than ever before. It is one of the major sources of protein on the globe.

Yet the British fried fish shop was nearly deprived of what its war time prime minister Winston Churchill called the battered fish's good companion - fried, chipped potatoes - by two other bedfellows, superstition and religious intolerance. Why, during an election campaign at Lewes on the English south coast in 1765, should one Protestant candidate have advocated 'No potatoes.

No Popery'? And why, across the sea in Ireland should one variety of potato have been dubbed 'the Protestant' by Catholics 'because we boil the devil out'? How on earth did this genial little tuber cause such offence? And what made Catholics more content with the crop than Protestants?

The reasons lie in 17th and 18th century Europe. During the early part of the period France was rising to prominence, eclipsing Spain (which had introduced the potato to Europe from its south American colonies) while England was embroiled in a civil war, many of its Protestant Separatists having set sail for America on board the Mayflower. The potato tuber was soon to reach them, carried in 1621 in a consignment of vegetables sent by the governor of Bermuda, Nathaniel Butler, to the English governor of Virginia at Jamestown, Francis Wyatt.

The nations left behind by the Pilgrim Fathers were troubled places, purged by puritans, wracked by religious dissent and plagued by superstition. Books were burned in the streets, churches sacked and country women drowned or hanged for their supposed bewitching ways - in 1686 Alice Molland from Exeter in England was executed for witchcraft. Beelzebub was believed to emerge as the sun set on parish and *clos*, and, accompanied by that witches' familiar the owl, set about curdling milk, souring bacon and burying his abominations in the kitchen garden: the potato. The vegetable, with its voluptuous curves, suggestive shapes and disturbing habit of multiplying in the cold ground, was clearly the work of the devil. And, as many observant Protestants noted, there was no mention of the potato in their bibles.

It did not help the potato's cause that the green fruit of the plant was highly toxic. (The English gardener John Evelyn, writing at the time, advocated eating the fruit pickled as a salad). Or that the potato, eaten raw, often caused an eczema-like condition which was thought to be a form of leprosy. Even as late as 1795 one David Davies was predicting that 'though the potato is an excellent root, deserving to be brought into general use, yet it seems not likely that the use of it should ever be normal in the country'.

He was mistaken. The Reverend Gilbert White observed in 1768: 'Potatoes have prevailed in this little district, by means of premiums, within these twenty years; and are much esteemed here now by the poor, who would scarce have ventured to taste them in the last reign.' White had been growing his potatoes for a decade: 'Planted 59 potatoes; not very large roots,' he wrote in his diary for 1758.

As a Protestant White might have noted how his Catholic colleagues were more tolerant of the vegetable provided it was ceremoniously planted on Good Friday and liberally sprinkled with Holy Water to keep any satanic influences at bay.

Yet the Germans, Protestant and Catholic alike, had already been won over by the potato. This followed a famine in Prussia when Frederick the Great (1712–1786) sent in free supplies of potatoes along with armed soldiers to persuade the peasantry to accept them. In 1853 the grateful citizens of Offenburg commissioned the sculptor Andreas Friederich to build a statue of Sir Francis Drake holding a potato plant in his hand. The base of the statue commemorated the fact that Drake 'introduced the potato to Europe in the year of our Lord 1586,' although, in reality, Spanish sailors had brought the little tubers home from South America at least two decades earlier. Friederich's statue stood in Offenburg town square until 1938 when, during the notorious anti-Jewish Kristallnacht riots, it was, inexplicably, torn down.

In neighbouring France the potato suffered a slow start even though, during the 1700s, the peasantry, struggling to survive in a boom and bust economy, could ill afford to be without it. In good years they survived. In poor years they starved on a diet of grass roots and ferns. Royal courtiers who tried to raise the issue before the king were scandalised by the callous response of Marie Antoinette, Louis XVI's queen consort: 'Qu'ils mangent de la brioche' - 'Let them eat cake.' (Whether the queen actually spoke these words remains in contention; the luxurious lifestyle of the royal family does not.) However a pharmacist, Antoine-Auguste Parmentier, had a better idea - 'Qu'ils mangent des pomme de terre'. Let them eat the earth apple or potato. As a former prisoner-of-war in Prussia Parmentier had survived the famine there on a diet of potatoes and he now campaigned vigorously for its adoption in his motherland. Parmentier tried trading on Marie Antoinette's vanity, persuading her to adorn her hair with the delicate, white potato flower. An alternative version has it that Louis himself wore a potato flower as a *boutonnière*. Whoever it was, the courtiers fawned in admiration and sought potato flowers for themselves.

The gourmets at court were further intrigued when Parmentier arranged a dinner at court where every course included *pomme de terre*. Then in 1770 Parmentier dealt Gallic prejudice to the potato the final *coup de grace* when King Louis allowed him use a field at Versailles to plant a top-secret crop of his precious *pomme de terre*. Guards were posted ostentatiously around the field to protect the crop while under instruction to ignore any thieving. The security arrangements doubled people's curiosity and, under the cover of darkness, the field was raided again and again. Citizens passed the illicit potato from hand to mouth.

The potato had arrived at last and, as if to emphasise the fact, French revolutionaries dug up the Tuileries Garden and planted them with potatoes in 1793, shortly after they had executed Louis XVI with Doctor Guillotine's admirable new invention. Parmentier

Fifty Tales from the Kitchen Garden

is celebrated still in French dishes such as *Hachis Parmentier*, a meal of minced beef covered with mashed potato.

In Britain the potato was beginning to receive a more favourable press. In 1838 William Cobbett (1763–1835) observed in *The English Gardener* that the potato 'does very well to qualify the effects of fat meat or to assist in the swallowing of quantities of butter. There appears to be nothing unwholesome about it, and when the sort is good, it is preferred by many people to some other vegetables of the coarser kind'. It was already offering salvation to those in the poorer, western highlands of the British Isles: in Wales, for example, the labourer owed a *dyled tato*, a potato debt, to the landowner who allowed him to grow his *tatws*.

Any vegetable that becomes central to the economy of a country soon develops its own customs, lexicon and traditions. This was nowhere more so than in Ireland. By the early 1900s Irish families were still sharing their meal of potatoes from the *skib*, the shallow wickerwork bowl which acquired a variety of poetical regional names including the scuttle (County Clare), the *ciseóg* (County Galway) and the sally saucer (County Louth). The spud, which seems to have acquired its nickname from the broad-pronged fork or 'spud' used to raise the crop, was eaten by Catholics and, eventually, by Protestants alike. Favourites included Epicure, Red Elephant and Champion, 'whilst Arran Banners were fed to the pigs,' reported author Olive Sharkey in her book *Common Knowledge*.

But by the late 1700s the escalating Irish population of eight million souls was putting severe pressure on the subsistence smallholders and their lazybeds of potatoes, planted on the bogland margins. The lazybed was a raised bed, 3.2 feet (1 metre) or three stalks wide, bordered by a narrow trench. The seed potato was cut in half and planted in March or April with a dibber or dibble. In Cavan and the midlands the dibber was known as a steeveen (from the Irish *stibhín*) and it was the job of the woman of the house who would let it be known that she was out 'guggering' (from *gogaire,* making holes for spuds). Earthing up or *lánú* where soil from the trench was scooped up and spread across the ridge was carried out three weeks after sowing and again a month later. The crop was regularly sprayed against blight with a mixture of bluestone and washing soda. Although the cause of blight was not yet understood the garden author James Shirley Hibberd hinted at who was to blame: 'Somebody sees it every year; it comes in autumn, it generally comes after wet weather, and *mark*, the most careless growers suffer the most from its attacks. But if some one now lamenting that he has lost half his crop, should rise up and say he bestowed every care upon it, I should say - "You didn't".'

Ironically the potato, a famine buster of a vegetable, proved a disaster for the Irish. The failure of the Irish potato crop in the 1840s was a national catastrophe and the subsequent famine killed a million and drove another two and a half million on to the emigration ships. Cobh near Cork, the port where the potato had first landed, was, for many Irish people, the final glimpse of home as the *cónra-long*, the coffin ships as they became known, bore them off on the twelve-week voyage across the Atlantic.

'When famine and disaster came upon that unhappy country its citizens took shelter under the Stars and Stripes,' wrote the garden author Edward A. Bunyard in *The Gardener's Companion* (1936) almost a century later. 'There they fanned the dying embers of hatred against the old country with a result that is with us today. No one... will regard a potato as a mere vegetable, but rather as an instrument of destiny.'

The potato had destroyed the heart of a nation: it was soon to transform the look of the countryside. Ireland's regime of inflated

Fifty Tales from the Kitchen Garden

rents, unmanageable mortgages and systematic evictions was unsustainable and, eventually, land reform saw almost three-quarters of the land redistributed among former tenants. While bankrupted owners abandoned their manor houses and walled kitchen gardens, large farm holdings were reorganised so that the fields formed a convenient series of rectangles spreading out behind the farmhouse, the so-called 'ladder farms,' still to be seen in parts of Ireland today.

The political potato had fuelled religious intolerance, saved nations from starvation and altered the lie of the land. It could also be said to be responsible for the fact that over 33 million Americans and almost a third of all Australians lay claim to Irish descent.

43. Veggies - A Class Act

Growing vegetables was always considered a useful occupation for the lower orders. The writing life of the English garden editor John Claudius Loudon spanned the industrial revolution, the era that turned most country people into a servile working class. And Loudon knew a thing or two about the improving effects of labouring in the kitchen garden. He offered this pearls-before-swine entry in his best selling 1822 *Encyclopaedia of Gardening*: 'In a state of labour and servitude, man is generally so dull and stupid, that almost every degree of refinement, or sensation beyond that of mere animal feeding, is lost on him.'

Loudon contrasts the brute-like worker with his more benevolent employer: 'The rich man is happily willing to put his hand in his pocket to help him; but that merely affords a temporary relief from evil.' The solution was simple, said Loudon. Proprietors should instruct their head gardeners to teach best husbandry to the local cottagers. In addition they should 'supply them with proper seed and plants, propagate a few fruit trees' and instruct the cottagers' wives on improved modes of cookery, for example by 'enlivening the soup with toasted crumbs of bread,

Fifty Tales from the Kitchen Garden

a few leaves of chives, and a half leaflet of green celery instead of boiling the ingredients *au naturel*'.

Once familiar with the healthy benefits of this *nouvelle cuisine*, the average working housewife might then benefit from the special discounts offered by kindly seed companies. This is from a Sutton Seed's spring catalogue of 1863:

'Seeds for distribution to cottagers. These are supplied at a reduction of about one-fourth from the Catalogue prices, with the view of assisting Clergymen and others who desire to encourage their Cottagers in the cultivation of their gardens. For this purpose we send the most useful kinds of Seeds only. Should any of our customers who desire to distribute Seeds among Cottagers not find it convenient to purchase them, we shall be glad to hear from them, in case we have any to spare free of charge.'

Loudon accepted that the lumbering labouring classes might need some persuasion since it was 'astonishing how ignorant and how extravagant the humblest classes are in these respects.' However, enforcing improvements with 'adequate motives of hope or fear, of reward or removal' would, he thought, prove a useful incentive and help spread happiness among the poorer households 'at no additional expense to the proprietor'.

In this manner 'wretchedness and slovenliness' in the workers' gardens would soon give way to gardens that were ornamental, neat and, above all, productive.

Loudon was not alone in his conviction that hands-on horticulture improved the body, the mind and the spirit, especially for members of the proletariat. The life of the high-minded Englishman John Ruskin (1819–1900) spanned the age of improvement that accompanied Queen Victoria's tenure of the British throne. He was a writer, critic, painter and a gardener and in 1871 he purchased, without inspecting it beforehand, a rambling country house, Brantwood, from his friend the Dean of Durham Cathedral. Brantwood overlooked the sparkling Coniston Water in Cumbria's Lake District and Ruskin was soon improving the view by removing the Dean's formal flower beds. They had been filled with what he described as foreign blooms 'pampered and bloated above their natural size [and] torn from the soil which they loved'. They were to be replaced with more naturalistic plantings since Ruskin wanted to adopt an organic approach to the gardens, one that was in harmony with the rugged Lake District surroundings and which celebrated what he considered the 'infinite wonderfulness ... in the flowers and the trees'. These botanical miracles were, as he put it, 'the means by which the earth becomes the companion of Man - his friend and his teacher.'

Ruskin was as deeply melancholic (his virgin wife Effy had recently eloped with the painter John Everett Millais for whom she had been modelling) as he was philanthropic and one of his lifelong projects was the St George's Company. Concerned that 'the British nation is at present unhealthy, poor' and alarmingly 'likely to perish,' the Company aimed to improve 'the health, wealth, and long life of the British nation.' The solution, Ruskin believed, was to aid the working man to return to the land and grow his own vegetables.

The organisation, later renamed the Guild of St George, was intended to benefit impoverished factory workers by liberating them from the tyranny of industrial machinery and helping them find instead healthy fulfilment in rustic labours. The new men and their families would thus be able to become stewards of the 'hills, streams and fields that God has made for us' and keep them as 'lovely, pure, and orderly as we can' as they 'gather their carefully cultivated fruit in one season'. Ruskin put £14,000 of his own money into the Guild in the expectation that the working

Fifty Tales from the Kitchen Garden

classes would enjoy significant social improvement. It would be especially helpful, he thought, if the beneficiaries might make 'scrupulous use of sugar-tongs instead of fingers.'

The Guild, always short of money, nevertheless managed to establish several rural communities of working people including one at Totley near Sheffield, another at Barmouth on the coast of mid Wales and a third at Bewdley in Worcestershire where Birmingham merchant George Baker had generously donated seven acres of Wyre Forest woodland to the Guild. (Baker would succeed Ruskin as Master of The Guild).

The land at Totley outside Sheffield was to be worked by a group of socialists who came together after Ruskin gave one of his anti-capitalist lectures at Ashfield in April 1876. St George's Farm, Totley, was set up as a communal enterprise under the auspices of William Hamilton Riley, a socialist and journalist recently returned from working in America. 'St George has now given thirteen acres of English ground for their own,' announced Ruskin trusting the families to rely on good work and 'no moving machines by fire' (Ruskin had a special loathing for steam engines). However the project faltered when Riley fell out with his fellow workers (he would return to America, settling in Massachusetts to earn a living as a socialist writer) leaving Ruskin dispatching his own head gardener at Brantwood, David Downs, to rescue the operation and turn Totley into a fruit farm.

The Barmouth project was more successful. The Guild had been given property by one of Ruskin's loyal admirers, Mrs Fanny Talbot. The necessary vegetable plots, however, were unproductive because of their exposure to driving westerly winds laden with salty sea spray. The wind and weather not only soured the soil, but played havoc with the buildings and Ruskin was obliged to devote substantial amounts of rental income to their repair. One of the Guild tenants, a French exile named Auguste Guyard, came up with a solution to the horticultural problem. Guyard was a curious figure. A radical utopian, he had been banished from his home village of Frotey near Vesoul in France by church leaders hostile to his plans to create a new socialist community there. Now, dressed in a grey cloak and wearing a startling red fez on his head, he would stride around his adopted home of Barmouth, frightening small children and dispensing useful advice including the suggestion that the vegetable gardens be protected with wind breaks 'fenced with furzed hedges'.

When Guyard died in 1882 grateful parishioners erected a tombstone over the grave inscribed:

Ci git un Semeur qui

Sema jusqu' au tombeau

Le Vrai, le Bien, le Beau

(Here lies a sower who/Until his death/Spread the seeds of /Truth, Goodness, and Beauty.)

Ruskin died in 1900. He went to his grave still convinced that working the kitchen garden was the best way to improve the human condition. There was little to show, however, that what Loudon called 'the humblest classes' exhibited any marked improvement in their behaviour.

44. John Loudon: Victorian Gardener

By the mid 1700s the science of horticultural was better advanced in England than anywhere in the world. It was still a world leader when John Claudius Loudon arrived in London, aged twenty, in 1803. He reached the capital during a period of social change that would transform his fortunes and the contents of the kitchen garden. In the manufacture of its engines, ships, cranes and bridges, the industrial age created a new breed of industrialists, a wealthy mercantile class eager for leisurely pursuits. Loudon would help them spend their money on gardens.

In appealing to the amateur gardener the canny author cast his net wide:

'Every man who does not limit the vegetable parts of his dinner to bread and potatoes, is a patron of gardening, by creating a demand for its productions,' he declared. 'He is a consumer, which is the first species of patron, and the more valuable varieties are such as regularly produce a dessert after dinner, and maintain throughout the year beautiful nosegays and pots of flowers in their lobbies and drawing rooms.'

Loudon had travelled to London meaning to set himself up as a landscape gardener, but he arrived with a letter of recommendation from a professor at Edinburgh University addressed to Sir Joseph Banks. Banks was an eminent man with a botanical knowledge to match the vast library in his Soho Square home. Thirty-five years earlier Banks had sailed with Captain Cook on the Endeavour, seen Botany Bay so named, and brought back a raft of new plants. A former scientific adviser to King George, he was now running the botanical gardens at Kew. He was the perfect introduction for the young, ambitious Mr Loudon.

Within a year of meeting Banks, Loudon had written his first book and over the next forty years Loudon wrote for the new, middle class market. When his books became 19th century best sellers, he founded his *Gardener's Magazine*, one of the early popular gardening periodicals in which he promised to 'record, as they occur, the various discoveries, acquisitions, and improvements that are constantly making in gardening ... and to render them available to practical men.' Furthermore, wrote the shrewd journalist, his magazine's advertising section would prove just the place to discover where to procure 'paints, cements, manures, [and] compositions for destroying insects such as Davidson's destroyer of earth worms.'

When in 1811 the sale of the lease on his Oxfordshire farm put £15,000 into Loudon's pocket, he set off across Europe to find out how those abroad managed their vegetable plots. 'The culinary vegetables of France have not been increased from the earliest period of horticultural history, with the exception of the sea-cale and the potatoe. In salading and legumes they far excel most countries; but in the cabbage tribe, turnips, and potatoes, they are inferior to the moister climates of Holland and Britain.'

Of Russia he wrote: 'the potatoe is but lately introduced, and that only in a few places. Many of the peasants refuse to eat or

Fifty Tales from the Kitchen Garden

cultivate this root, from mere prejudice, and from an idea very natural to a people in a state of slavery, that any thing proposed by their lords must be for the lord's advantage, and not theirs; thus the first handful of food thrown to untamed animals operates as a scare.' In Italy, things were little better. 'Italian cucumbers are never so succulent as those grown in our humid frames by dung-heat. The love-apple, egg-plant, and capsicum, are extensively cultivated near Rome and Naples for the kitchen; the fruit of the first attaining a larger size, and exhibiting the most grotesque forms.'

The Mediterraneans, it seemed, had moved on little since the collapse of the Roman empire: 'Of culinary vegetables the Italians began with those left them by the Romans, and they added the potatoe to their number as soon as, or before, we did.

'Though the Italians have the advantage over the rest of Europe in fruits, that good is greatly counterbalanced by the inferiority of their culinary vegetables.'

Loudon never travelled to America, but he gleaned enough details from publications such as seedsman B. McMahon's American Kalendar to comment: 'Culinary vegetables grow in the same perfection as in England, excepting the cauliflower and some species of beans. Water-melons, musk-melons, squashes, sweet potatoes, cucumbers, &c. arrive at great perfection.' The growing of squash was of particular interest: 'The seeds of pumpkin are scattered in the field, when planting the corn, and no further trouble is necessary than throwing them into the wagon when ripe.'

John Claudius Loudon died in December 1843. It was the end of an era, but one in which the cause of the common vegetable had been well advanced.

45. War Winning Vegetables

Towards the end of the First World War many British people were becoming very, very hungry. Those with the money to pay the soaring cost of black market food ate well enough. However a German blockade of shipping supplies proved so effective that Britain was forced to fall back on its own resources. Old grazing pastures and milk meadows were put to the plough to grow wheat for bread and the government dithered over whether to introduce food rationing: with almost every community mourning its war dead, adding rationing to their woes was judged to be politically imprudent. Eventually however, in 1918, flour, meat, sugar, milk and butter were all strictly rationed.

By now there were food riots in Austrian Hungary, Turkey and Russia, the latter stoking up the civil unrest that would lead to the Russian Revolution. On the streets of Berlin fights would break out over a handful of potato peelings. There were food shortages in the US too. When the price of a New York onion rose by 700% some housewives took to the streets to protest: many more turned to their gardens to grow their own. Public parks, golf courses and vacant lots fell to hoe and spade in a patriotic wave

Fifty Tales from the Kitchen Garden

of community gardening. Posters exhorted the nation to 'Sow The Seeds of Victory'. It was the first time in American history that the message went out: eating greens does you good. As President Woodrow Wilson led the nation to war against Germany on April 6 1917, he told the people: 'Everyone who creates or cultivates a garden helps. This is a time for America to correct her unpardonable fault of wastefulness and extravagance.'

The National War Garden Commission issued posters declaring 'Every Garden a Munition Plant' and offered free books on gardening, canning and drying. 'Can Vegetables and Fruit - and Can The Kaiser Too' read another poster. The unrestrained enthusiasm for turning every available piece of greenery into a vegetable plot was not shared by all. The Department of Agriculture regarded the work of the War Gardens agency as amateur interference into what was properly the province of the farmers. Yet despite their lobbying the United States School Garden Army had enrolled 1.5 million children when the war came to an end in 1918.

France, too, set to work on its public *potager*. The French emperor and military strategist Napoleon Bonaparte (1769–1821) had once remarked that an army marches on its stomach and, as if to prove his point, the gardens of the grand Palace of Versailles were turned over to vegetables. In 1917 25 million leek seeds were sown in place of the formal flowers at the Palace. When they were large enough to be transplanted, the seedlings were lifted and ferried in military trucks to the Front where they could be replanted close behind the Allied army lines to be grown on and finally fed to the fighting troops.

War-torn Britain was also busy with its private and public vegetable gardens. Under DORA, the Defence of the Realm Act, local government requisitioned land in order to increase the number of garden allotments from 600,000 to 1.5 million. A campaign, dubbed Every Man A Gardener, was mounted and the King, who had hastily changed the Germanic family name from Saxe-Coburg-Gotha to the more English Windsors, patriotically ordered the decorative geraniums in the flower beds facing Buckingham Palace to be replaced with potatoes and cabbages. The Church of England gave special dispensation for its congregations to work the land on Sundays (although many conservative farmers stoutly refused to allow ploughing on the Sabbath). It prompted one Revd E.H. Archer-Shepherd to suggest that Sunday work was better than leaving young men 'hanging about the lanes in groups, waiting for Satan to find some mischief for idle hands'.

By the end of the war, the nation had stepped up to produce a startling two million tons of fresh vegetables. By November 11 1918, even as the lawns of London's Kew gardens yielded nearly 30 tons of potatoes, the Germans surrendered.

Both sides exchanged their prisoners of war and internees. Among those returned to Britain were internees from Ruhleben. At the outbreak of the war Germany had arrested all British men aged between 17 and 55 then in their country and imprisoned four thousand of them on the ten-acre racecourse at Ruhleben outside Berlin. German soldiers patrolled the perimeter while the camp prisoners, having been left to regulate themselves, set up a camp magazine and established sporting teams and clubs including a horticultural society. One Thomas Howat was nominated secretary and he wrote to the Royal Horticultural Society in London requesting formal affiliation, but warning that he might have a problem paying any subscriptions due.

Ruhleben was a barren place and liable to flooding. Howat explained in his letter of application that his club intended to 'cultivate and beautify the ground around the barracks and public thoroughfares in the Lager, and to further the knowledge of

Fifty Tales from the Kitchen Garden

horticulture'. The Royal Society approved his application and sent seeds, bulbs and instructional gardening pamphlets for the use of prisoners, men like David Tulloch, a crofter's boy from Speyside who knew nothing about gardening. He had been at sea all his life and was serving as engineer on board SS Rubislaw when war broke out and his ship was impounded. He now became one of the club's 943 members, attending the Society's winter lectures and toiling away on the vegetable gardens, which not only improved the diet of the internees, but, in 1917, turned a profit of 800 marks.

In 1918 Tulloch and many thousands of wounded soldiers returned to nurse their injuries and recover from shell shock by cultivating fruits and vegetables on allotments: the rest and recuperative value of gardening was seen as especially important to returning servicemen.

In the US by the mid 1920s the backyard kitchen gardening movement was once again in decline, partly because of food surpluses and partly because of the invention of an Irishman whose family had been driven from their home during the potato famine. This was Henry Ford, the man who popularised the horseless carriage, a machine that, within a decade, saw off the daily deposit of over 1,000 tons of horse manure on the streets of New York. The manure had been enough to enrich every garden in the city. The European and American economic depression of the 1930s triggered another war, this time against poverty. Once again there was a revival of the kitchen garden movement as townspeople started soup kitchens, distributing penny portions of bread and soup to the poor. As Americans took a closer look at subsistence gardening and British publishers marketed *Shilling Guides* on cottage cookery, there was a minor land rush by families who preferred to put their trust in Mother Nature rather than the factory assembly line. Already, however, another war was looming.

46. Dig for Victory

During the 1930s in town and country, Sunday morning was traditionally the time when the men folk tended their allotments and kitchen gardens. One September Sunday in 1939, however, the gardens were silent. Instead householders across France and Britain waited by their wirelesses to discover whether Germany would respond to a joint ultimatum to withdraw its invasion troops from Poland. The German leader Hitler had sent in his troops and bombed Warsaw, Katowice, Krakow, Tczew and Tunel. The British prime minister, Neville Chamberlain, came on air shortly after an informative programme on making a meal from canned foods: 'I have to tell you,' he said, his speech strained, 'that no such undertaking has been given and that consequently this country is at war with Germany.' Within minutes air raid sirens sounded across London in what turned out to be a false alarm and, for the next seven months, what the French called the *drôle de guerre*, the funny war, began. Nations prepared to wage war with weapons. And their kitchen gardens.

In America national food surpluses had broken all previous records. Although nitrogen was more profitably turned into explosives than garden fertiliser, and although there was a perceived need to grow more food, the Agriculture Department

Fifty Tales from the Kitchen Garden

campaigned against any move to 'plow up the parks and the lawns to grow vegetables'. Their lobbying was only partly successful: when in 1942 the Burpee Victory Garden Seed Packet went on sale, seed trade trebled. In 1943 as canned food was put on rations, president Franklin D. Roosevelt ordered the White House lawn to be dug up and planted with cabbages, carrots, beans and tomatoes. Around four million Americans joined the grow-your-own vegetable brigade.

Having learned their lesson during the First World War, the British government introduced food rationing early on. By January 1940 households had to register at local shops for their supplies of bacon, ham, butter and sugar. Soon all basic foodstuffs were rationed and the government began a campaign to turn the people into a nation of kitchen gardeners. 'Half a million more allotments properly worked will provide potatoes and vegetables that will feed another million adults and one and a half million children for eight months of the year, so lets get going and let Dig For Victory be the matter for everyone with a garden or allotment,' declared Lord Woolton, the agricultural minister.

Eleanour Sinclair Rohde (1881–1950), the English gardening author who had been largely responsible for promoting the modern herb garden, settled down instead to write *The Wartime Vegetable Garden*. The agriculture ministry meanwhile circulated cropping plans for a 'ten-rod' allotment, running Dig For Victory exhibitions and setting up demonstration vegetable plots in towns and villages. Every school in Britain was encouraged to tend its own vegetable patch. It was a move that not only produced more food, but also resulted in a post-war generation of vegetable gardeners, moulded from wartime pupils tending their 'tators and peas'.

Vegetables acquired a premium. Home guardsmen in London optimistically made hand grenades from potatoes with slivers

Bill Laws

of razor blades embedded in the skin. There were recipes for War And Peace pudding (made with flour, breadcrumbs, suet, mixed fruit and a cupful of grated carrot), carrot croquettes, carrot fudge, and cake mixtures made with mashed potatoes. There was Potato Pete's recipe book and Woolton Pie, named after the British government minister and made with potatoes, parsnips and herbs. There were mock potato omelettes, mock hamburgers and mock duck, the latter made with mashed potatoes, lentils, beans, sage and onions and shaped, mockingly, like a duck. Vegetable scraps were collected in the street and fed to community pigs raised by neighbourhood pig clubs to supplement the meat rations.

Soldiers and civilians throughout Europe became nervous, hungry, but healthy: 'Most people are better fed than they used to be. There are less fat people,' observed the writer George Orwell at the time. People would never be so healthy again.

As Britain's Dig For Victory campaign was launched in October 1939, Sir John Anderson, the man in charge of air raid precautions, gave his name to the little corrugated iron bomb shelters that people buried in their gardens beneath their precious vegetable patches. The government once again used emergency powers to increase the number of allotments to 1.4 million and banned their use for the growing of ornamental flowers. Americans donated 90 tons of vegetable seed and shipped them over to the British allotment holders. By 1942 patriotic gardeners was estimated to be producing a record breaking 1.3 million tons of fresh food. Even the green sward covering the moat around one of London's tourists' hotspots, the Tower of London, was dug up and turned into vegetable plots by the Tower workers.

Aerial warfare did not improve the safety of the wartime vegetable garden, especially for those whose homes lay beneath hostile air corridors. One housewife living at Farnham in Surrey, England recalled: 'I was out in the garden and I could see this plane coming in. I knew it was a different one to ours from the sound of it. And next thing, there was a line of washing out, about three doors away, and he came down and he peppered all the sheets with the machine gun!' She added with satisfaction: 'They brought him down two miles out of Aldershot and then he was put on view. Sixpence to go and have a look at him.' It was a contravention of the Geneva Convention on the treatment of prisoners of war, but understandable in the circumstances.

In 1941 London's Royal Horticultural Society published *The Vegetable Garden Displayed* and five years later it was translated into German and shipped overseas to help in the post-war reconstruction of Europe's vegetable gardens. Did vegetables win the war? No, but they certainly made people feel better. When canned foods came off the ration list America's wartime gardeners could afford to relax. Yet vegetable seed sales continued to grow along with the suburban garden movement. In the early 1950s 39% of American families still grew much of their own vegetables and gardening remained the nation's most popular hobby, thanks to those wartime kitchen gardeners.

47. Vegetable Radicals

A garden is a lovesome thing, God wot! announced the English Victorian Thomas Edward Brown in his poem, *My Garden*. Yet the garden, and the kitchen garden in particular, could inspire political unrest. Aside from using vegetables as the instrument of protest (during the middle ages in Europe it was common practise to pelt miscreants with rotten vegetables) growing them as a form of protest has a long and respectable past. After being bankrupted by the English Civil War the clothier and political activist Gerrard Winstanley was reduced to herding cattle for a living. He was outraged by the poverty he saw around him and in 1649 he and his community of 'Diggers' or True Levellers invaded a patch of common land and proceeded to dig it up and plant vegetables. 'In Cobham on the little heath the digging still goes on and all our friends, they live in love as if they were but one,' he rhymed.

Oliver Cromwell, the Lord Protector who had defeated the Royalists during the Civil War, sent in soldiers to deal with this vegetable protest and destroy the diggers' parsnips, carrots and beans. Another nine colonies suffered a similar fate. Winstanley

Fifty Tales from the Kitchen Garden

appealed to Cromwell, the self proclaimed champion of honest people, pointing out that it was foolish and short-sighted to neglect the poor: 'If the wasteland of England were manured by her children it would become in a few years the richest, the strongest and the most flourishing country in the world,' claimed Winstanley. And, he said, if all the impoverished people in the land were well fed and made healthy they would soon be 'making discoveries to benefit all'. The radical digger went on to promote the concept of a free state health service. Three centuries later his country became the world's first to adopt such a scheme, but in the 1600s Winstanley's pleas were ignored and when Cromwell was defeated and the rule of the monarchy re-imposed, Winstanley slipped from view and died in obscurity.

Three hundred and fifty years later in 1995 a group of protestors calling themselves This Land is Ours headed into Surrey to reoccupy St George's Hill, the site of the Digger's first vegetable patch. Their plan, to erect a memorial stone to Winstanley, led to clashes with the authorities.

There had already been other land protest during the 1970s when supporters of the environmental campaign group Friends of the Earth organised demonstration 'dig-ins' on empty plots of land. They were protesting about the national shortage of allotments. There were still 121,000 people on allotment waiting lists in 1980 when different demonstrations began, this time against the siting of American cruise missiles in the UK. While women set up protest peace camps at an American air base, Greenham Common, Chris Mattingly, the husband of one protester, loaded his old Massey Ferguson tractor and plough onto the back of a trailer and set off for RAF Mildenhall, another American air base in the county of Suffolk. Under the bewildered surveillance of the military guards he unloaded his tractor, hitched up the plough and turned a symbolic acre of land at the base. He returned later and sowed a crop of wheat which, in late summer, was harvested, threshed and presented to one of the aid agencies for export to a famine-struck region in the developing world, Bangladesh.

Mattingly's protest came at the point in time when the digital revolution was gathering pace. Ten years earlier (and 60 years since the world's first official airmail service had started at Uttar Pradesh in India) Ray Tomlinson sent himself a test email at Cambridge Massachusetts. It was the world's first. Yet even as technology was scaling extraordinary new heights, millions of people continued to die of hunger.

Concerned by their plight and by the impact of agribusiness and genetic modification on global seed stocks, a Frenchman called Dominique Guillet began rescuing old varieties of vegetable seed in 1994. After a spell making products for the Bach Flower Remedy company, founded in Wales in 1930 and devoted to the craft of homeopathy, he started growing old vegetable varieties on an estate in the Auvergne. His company, Terre de Semences, was dedicated to *'la libération de la semence et de l'humus,'* the liberation of seeds and humus, but he was forced to shut down the company (and establish a seed library instead) when the French Ministry of Agriculture demanded a registration fee for each of Terre de Semences' 2,000 seeds. This was despite a European Union directive on promoting the production of traditional vegetable varieties and the fact that, in the course of a century, the west had lost 98% of its vegetable varieties.

'Let us not speak of transgenic plants: one page would not suffice to express our anger,' wrote Guillet. 'To find and ask the true questions we would need a whole book and we have not got the time or space. We have far too much to do on the land so as to produce honest seeds so that growers can regain their freedom and their choice.'

Terre de Semences was followed in 1999 by Association Kokopelli, an organisation devoted to saving old varieties and distributing seed, free if possible, to the developing world. Within its first two years Kokopelli had distributed 150,000 seed packets in Asia, Africa and South America.

48. Monstrous Vegetables

A modest little pumpkin festival was founded in 1986 at downtown Port Elgin on the banks of Lake Huron in Ontario, Canada. The first weigh off attracted several pumpkins up to 250 pounds (113 kilograms), but by 2011 38-year-old Ontarian Joel Jarvis weighed in with a giant: at just over 1485 pounds (674 kilograms) it was a monster.

The eccentric and distracted Lord Emsworth held similar ambitions for his Hope of Blandings. This was the fictional pumpkin and the star of P.G. Wodehouse's story, *The Custody of the Pumpkin*, first published in the *Saturday Evening Post* in 1924 to the delight of its American readers. They learned how Emsworth and his head gardener Angus McAllister finally took the top prize for the gargantuan pumpkin at the annual Shrewsbury Show in Shropshire from Emsworth's rival and neighbour, Sir Gregory Parsloe-Parsloe.

Both of these pumpkin stories celebrate the success of the horticultural show, events which ranged from top hat and tail coat affairs attended by royalty, to parish fetes patronised by the lord, his labourer and everyone in between. The horticultural

Fifty Tales from the Kitchen Garden

show gave working people the chance to forget their work-a-day lives for a while. They might enter the country craft competition, egg painting in Moldavia or corn dolly making in Cornwall. They might compete for a prize for the fastest plait of a string of onions in Brittany or tossing a caber in Ontario. They might even find romance. The following was inscribed in neat copper plate handwriting in the flyleaf of a 1896 programme from the Shrewsbury Horticultural Show: "Preserved by Annie Lewis. In loving memory of the day in which I first met my husband David C. Lewis. Married August 9th 1897."

At the heart of every fruit and vegetable show, however, was size whether it involved the longest pole bean, the pod with most peas, the knobbliest squash or the fattest onion. The battle to become vegetable champion inevitably involved some heinous activities. Even in quiet country villages the threat of sabotage or theft led anxious growers to mount a midnight guard over their prize monsters.

Keith Ruck, a former head gardener at a Herefordshire manor house and, like his father before him, a horticultural show judge, revealed some of the secrets behind becoming a prize winning vegetable grower. 'There was a lot of cheating went on. Like if you got wireworm in a carrot, you take some soap and an old carrot, mush him up to get the right blend of colour and then use that to cure the blemish. Course when I was judging I used to look out for things like that because I knew how it was done.'

During the 1920s Ruck's father regularly took gold medals in the Cottagers' Class at Shrewsbury where the fictitious Lord Emsworth had won his pumpkin victory. 'A lot of parsnips were grown in barrels, in holes barred down through the soil and filled with leaf mould and sand so the parsnips didn't have to fight against anything,' Ruck recalled. 'During the shows then, the parsnips would be rested in the old bungalow baths, or zinc baths, laid on damp sacking.' Judges looked for length as well as an unblemished skin. 'The parsnips were the full length of the bath and some of the tapering ends would be hanging over the top of the bath.'

But the showman's garden, he remembered, was not an orderly place. 'We never had a tidy garden. You got leeks growing in pipes, kidney beans growing in wire cages so they would grow nice and straight, and we were always digging into the rows so you never had anything perfect to look at.'

The growing of prize onions had a particularly deleterious effect on the look and the smell of the garden. 'The show onions were started in the winter, in seed. Growing onions was a sore point with my mother because one of Dad's friends was a butcher from Abergavenny who done his own slaughtering. We used have drums of blood and we'd soak the ground with it 'til it go near a green or a black colour. It didn't used to smell very sweet either.'

First thing in the morning and last thing at night his father would hoe the onions. 'His chief aim was to get the air to them,' Keith explained. And it worked. 'Father took hundreds of prizes.'

By the end of the 20th century record-breaking vegetable growers competed for an entry in the Guinness Book of Records. One of the consistently successful monster makers was Bernard Lavery of Llanharry in Wales who, at one stage, held nineteen world records and 10 British records for growing giant vegetables. He grew a cabbage that weighed 123.9 pounds (56.24 kilograms), a marrow of 108 pounds (49.04 kilograms), a 28 pound (12.73 kilogram) radish; a 20 pound (9.10 kilogram) cucumber, a 18.1 pound (8.25 kilogram) Brussel sprout and, in 1996, a carrot that weighed 11.4 pounds (5.20 kilograms). Other growers continued the potentially expensive quest for monster vegetables: in 2016 Essex's Matthew Oliver revealed that he had paid £1,250 (1,559

Fifty Tales from the Kitchen Garden

US dollars) for the seed that produced a giant squash weighing over 1330 pounds (603.2 kilogram).

For giant vegetable growers the attraction amounted to more than the mere pursuit of prizes. In Alaska where the short growing season (105 days on average) was compensated by the length of the summer days vegetable growers exhibiting at the Palmer State Fair, northeast of Anchorage, earned a reputation for producing horticultural giants. They ranged from 138 pound (62.5 kilogram) cabbages to a 65 pound (29.4 kilogram) cantaloupe. One grower, interviewed by the local media, agreed that the pursuit of excellence involved long hours and deep determination. But, he added philosophically: 'If you're growing outside, you're growing inside'.

49. Artists and their Kitchen Gardens

Gardeners often look on artists as a potentially inspiring group of horticulturalists. Being creative individuals, artists can usually be relied upon to apply the same visual and conceptual gifts to their gardens as they do to their art. Those expectations were fully realised in Claude Monet (1840–1926) whose Normandy garden Giverny became one of the world's most famous. Monet shared his horticultural enthusiasms with another painter Gustave Caillebotte (1848–1894). When Monet and Caillebotte proposed visiting a friend, the friend wrote back to Monet: 'I'm glad you are bringing Caillebotte. We'll talk about gardening since Art and Literature are nonsense. Earth is the only thing that matters.'

The earth, especially that which lay beneath his *potager*, mattered greatly to Monet. He was a *bon viveur* who, like many French patriarchs, demanded fresh vegetables at the table. As his paintings began to sell well, he bought another house at Giverny in the neighbouring Rue de Chêne, simply for its walled kitchen garden. It was also equipped with forcing frames, a

Fifty Tales from the Kitchen Garden

cellar for storage and mushroom growing, and a fertile soil for his turnips, tomatoes, peppers and beans.

Monet was a prodigious painter who worked from dawn to dusk, but he would take time out every day to visit his vegetable garden on the Rue de Chêne and select the produce that was to be picked first thing the following day and served at the family's supper table.

His Impressionist colleague Pierre-Auguste Renoir (1841–1919), meanwhile, was overseeing the planting of his own kitchen garden in Provençe. In 1906, an ancient olive grove on a smallholding, Les Collettes near Cagnes-sur-Mer, was due to be cut down and replaced with a market garden. Prompted by the threat to the old trees, Renoir bought Les Collettes. (According to his son, the film-maker Jean Renoir, the painter was an instinctive conservationist who would take care not to tread on even the humble *pis-en-lit*, the diuretic dandelion, when out for a walk.) The painter created a studio within the garden and while he worked, Aline, his former model and lover and now the mother of his three children, laboured in their kitchen garden. She manured the soil with grape skins and dung from her goat, rabbits and hens, and paid special attention to their semi-permanent artichoke beds. And when the time came she always made sure the first pressing from the old olives at Les Collettes was ceremoniously presented to her husband.

Monet and Renoir were self-made men. Renoir had worked as an impoverished apprentice in a Parisian porcelain factory when he was 13 while Monet had laboured hard and long before his paintings started to sell for serious money. Their mutual friend Gustave Caillebotte, however, was born with the proverbial silver spoon in his mouth thanks to his father Martial's success in the linen business. They lived at Cain, a grand house set in ten hectares of land near the old bridge in Verres, about twenty kilometres from Paris.

Caillebotte's popularity as a painter seemed to wane in proportion to his consuming passion for gardening although when, on the death of his mother Céleste, Gustave and his brother inherited the property, the painter executed over 80 works of the house and gardens. Among them were *The Kitchen Garden, The Park at Yerres, The Wall of the Kitchen Garden* and *The Gardeners* (1875–1877), which pictured two bare-foot men in rolled up britches and sun hats drenching a neat row of haricot beans in the whitewashed walled kitchen garden. Here Caillebotte, who also raised rare orchids, experimented with planting arrangements, putting to the test the theories of Michel-Eugène Chevreul (1786–1889): Chevreul's critical analysis of colour and his notions about complementary colours had profoundly influenced the Impressionist painters and would later influence the work of the painter turned garden designer, Gertrude Jekyll. As with Monet's and Renoir's gardens, Caillebotte's family estate at Yerres was preserved and restored for posterity, even down to the walled garden which was taken over and managed by the *Potager Caillebotte*.

Other French Impressionists enjoyed the fruits of their vegetable patch, on both canvass and the kitchen table. It influenced Impressionists elsewhere in Europe and America to set up their easels in the kitchen garden as with William Merrit Chase (1849–1916) and his *A Visit to the* Garden (1890). Those who failed to follow the trend risked losing popular appeal. Václar Brožik (1851–1901) was regarded as one of the most talented of the Czech artists, but his evocative *Evening Return from the Field*, which depicted a couple wending their way home past the cottage cabbage and pumpkin patch, looked distinctly old fashioned beside *The Artist's Garden at Eragny* or *Vegetable Garden*

Fifty Tales from the Kitchen Garden

at L'Hermitage near Pontoise by Camille Pissarro (1830–1903). This fresh flood of light on the canvass took an exuberant step forward with such works as *Vegetable Garden with Donkey* painted by the Catalan surrealist Joan Miro in 1918 on a farm near Tarragona.

Many other more moderate artists took the kitchen garden as their theme. The Scottish artist Arthur Melville (1855–1904), hailed as one of the most original painters of his time, made a name, and a profit, for himself by selling *A Cabbage Garden*, his debut painting for London's Royal Academy Show in 1878. The oil painting depicted a grizzled gardener conversing with a young lady as he weeded cabbages in the kale yard. Helen Allingham also looked at the *potager*. Her watercolours of rustic cottages adorned with roses and hollyhocks made her the darling of the Victorian age (she had been trying to capture the country scenes before they were swept away by Londoners moving out of town and gentrifying the neighbourhood). Allingham's *Cutting Cabbages* (1884), however, portrayed a sad, demure child, cabbage in one hand, cutting knife in the other. It echoed a work by James Guthrie (1859–1930) in his bleak *A Hind's Daughter* (a hind was a skilled labourer). Guthrie pictured the girl with her cabbage and knife looking distinctly displeased by her occupation.

The Pompeiian house painter who pictured Priapus weighing his penis against a bowl of fruit and vegetables provided what is perhaps the sauciest representation of the garden harvest. However the strangest vegetable representations were those of the 16th century artist Giuseppe Arcimboldo. Little was known about the artist. He was born in Milan in 1527 and at 38 became a painter at the royal courts of the Hapsburgs. Arcimboldo, judging from his representational self-portraits, was a good-looking fellow, but he pursued a peculiar obsession with vegetables

217

 Bill Laws

when he turned to the portraiture of others, in particular those of his patron, Rudolph II. Arcimboldo had already trialled these curious vegetable portraits under the patronage of Maximilian II in 1569. In his final commission in 1591, two years before his death, Arcimboldo painted an allegorical portrait of Rudolph where the monarch's face was composed entirely of vegetables and fruits. His patron was said to have been delighted with the result.

If Arcimboldo seemed unconventional by comparison, there was always the work of Heather and Ivan Morison. Their *Colours and Sounds in Ivan Morison's Garden* (2002) consisted of an installation and DVD that celebrated the couple's allotment in Birmingham, England. At one point the camera focused on a hanging kettle, the head of a rake and the artist Ivan Morison standing by the greenhouse, naked but for his sun hat.

50. Villandry

The château at Villandry is one of a rash of country houses that line the Loire valley in France. When a successful Spanish physician Dr Joachim Carvallo (1869–1936) took over the restoration of its formal gardens in the early 1900s, aided on the expenses side by his marriage to a wealthy Pennsylvanian heiress, he created one of the world's most decorative vegetable gardens.

Designed to be viewed from the high windows of the château or the vine-covered raised walk that surrounded the garden, Carvallo arranged for the restoration of Villandry's 18th century gardens basing his work on the engravings of French manor gardens from the 1600s by Jacques Androuet du Cerceau.

There was the Jardin d'Ornement designed by a Spanish artist Lozano to symbolise four stages of love, its box hedges enclosing plants to suggest hearts, flames, masks, fans and dagger blades (for *l'amour tragique*). Then there was the Jardin d'Eau, an ornamental basin connected to a canal and filled with carp. But the glory of the garden was the Jardin Potager, a feature that draws visitors from around the world.

Separated from the Jardin d'Ornement by an avenue of limes, the Jardin Potager was constructed of nine square quarters, each with its own geometric parterre and hedged with

 Bill Laws

low-growing box. Carvallo filled his parterres not with lavish blooms, stately shrubs, or coloured stones, but with every-day French vegetables - over 30,000 of them. Packed together in a maze-like design, there were ruby chard and tomatoes, decorative cabbage and carrots, basil, aubergines and black pimiento. Dr Joachim Carvallo had created the world's most spectacular ornamental potager.

Further Reading

The vegetable world is filled with wonderful writings from the 1600s onwards. I am indebted to all those authors who have already followed the vegetal trail - and recommend them to any wishing to continue along it.

Amos, Sharon, *Thriving In The Garden* (Country Living magazine, September 2002)

Baeyer, Edwina von and Crawford, Pleasance, *Garden Voices: two centuries of Canadian Garden Writing* (Random House of Canada, 1997)

Bareham, Lindsey, *In Praise of the Potato* (Grafton Books, 1991)

Barkas, Janet, *The Vegetable Passion* (Routledge, Kegan and Paul, 1975)

Batchelor, John, *There is no wealth but life* (Chatto and Windus, 2000)

Beale, Catherine, *Hampton Court: A Brief History* (Hampton Court Estate, 2000)

Berrall, Julia S. *The Garden An Illustrated History*, (Penguin Books, 1978)

Blunt, Wilfred, *The Compleat Naturalist - A Life of Linnaeus* (Frances Lincoln, 2001)

Boff, Charles, *The Big Book of Gardening* (Odhams Press)
Briffa, Dr. John, *I Can See Clearly Now* (Observer Magazine, August 25, 2002)
Briffa, Dr. John, *It Won't End In Tears* (Observer Magazine, April 27, 2002)
Brown, Jane *The Pursuit of Paradise* (Harper Collins, 1999)
Bunyard, E.A, *The Gardeners Companion* (J.M.Dent, 1936)
Campbell, Susan, *Charleston Kedding,* (Ebury Press, 1996)
Carroll, Maureen, *They came, they saw, they conquered* (RHS Journal, The Garden, June 2003)
Crouch, David and Ward, Colin, *The Allotment* (Faber, 1988)
Dannatt, Adrian, *Undercover Agent* (The Guardian June 7 2003)
Davies, Jennifer *The Wartime Kitchen And Garden* (BBC Books 1993)
Devonshire, The Duchess of, *The Garden At Chatsworth* (Frances Lincoln 1999
Dickens, Charles, *Dombey and Sons* (Knopf, 1994)
Don, Monty, *Eat With Beet,* (Observer Magazine, February 9 2003)
Drower, George, *Gardeners, Gurus and Grubs – The Stories of Garden Inventors and*
Innovations (Sutton Publishing 2001)
Ducas, Jane, *The Complete Works of Nature,* (Weekend Telegraph, January 15 2000)
Dudley, Stuart, *Taking The Ache Out Of Gardening* (The Garden Book Club, 1962)
Dyer, Christopher, *Everyday Life in Medieval England* (Hambledon and London, 1994)
Garmey, Jane, *The Writer In The Garden,* (Algonquin Books of Chapel Hill, 1999)
Green, Candida Lycett and Lawson, Andrew, *Brilliant Gardens* (Chatto & Windus 1989)

Fifty Tales from the Kitchen Garden

Griffiths, Mark, *The Times A Century in Photographs - Gardening* (Times Books, 2000)
Grigson, Jane, *The Vegetable Book* (Penguin Books 1980)
Guillet, Dominique, *The Seeds of Kokopelli* (Association Kokopelli, 2002)
Hadfield, Miles, Editor, *The Gardener's Companion* (J.M.Dent 1936)
Hamilton, Geoff, *Successful Organic Gardening,* (Dorling Kindersley, 1987)
Hanawalt, B *The Ties That Bound*, (OUP 1986)
Hellyer, Arthur, *The Shell Guide to Gardens,* (Book Club Associates, 1977)
Hellyer, A. G. L. *The Amateur Gardener* (W. H. & L. Collingridge, 1948)
Hibberd, Shirley, *Profitable Gardening* (Groombridge & Son)
Hills, Lawrence D. *Comfrey, Past Present & Future* (Faber)
Hills, Lawrence D. *Organic Gardening* (Penguin Books, 1977)
Hills, Lawrence D. *Fighting Like the Flowers* – The life story of Britain's best-known organic gardener (ISBN: 1 870098 30 7)
Huxley, Anthony, *An Illustrated History of Gardening* (Paddington Press, 1983)
Jay, Roni *Sacred Gardens,* (Thorsons, 1998)
King, Ronald, *The Quest for Paradise* (Whittet Books 1979)
Landsberg, Sylvia, *The Medieval Garden* (Thames and Hudson, 1996)
Lawrence, Elizabeth, *Gardening For Love* (Duke University Press, 1987)
Lawrence, W.J.C. *Catch The Tide* (*Adventures in Horticultural Research*, (Grower Books, 1980)
Laws, Bill, *Artists' Gardens,* (Ward Lock, 1999)
Loudon, J.C., *An Encyclopaedia of Gardening* (Longman, Rees, Orme, Brown and Green, 1826)

Lovelock, Yann, *The Vegetable Book – An Unnatural History* (George, Allen & Unwin, 1972)
McQuillan, Dan, *Queen of spuds,* (Sainsbury's Magazine, October 2002)
Maybe, Richard, *Flora Britannica* (Sinclair-Stevenson, 1996)
Morgan, Joan and Richards, Alison *A Paradise out of a Common Field* (Random Century Group 1990)
Mountain, D. (Thomas Hill), *The Gardeners Labyrinth 1594* (Garland Publishing Inc, 1982)
Moynahan, Brian, *The British Century* (Weidenfeld & Nicolson, 1997)
Parkinson, John, *A Garden of Pleasant Flowers,1629* (Dover Publications, 1976)
Pears, Pauline (Editor in chief) *Encyclopedia of Organic Gardening* (Dorling Kindersley
Potter, Beatrix *The Tale of Peter Rabbit* (F.Warne & Co., 1902)
Pudney, John *The Smallest Room* (Michael Joseph 1954
Rackham, Oliver, *The History of the Countryside* (J.M.Dent, 1986)
Roberts, Jonathon, *Cabbages and Kings; The origins of Fruit and Vegetables* (Collins, 2001)
Roddick, Anita *Take It Personally* (Thorsons, 2001)
Saunders, Nicholas, *Alternative England and Wales* (Nicholas Saunders, 1975)
Seymour, John *The Complete Book of Self Sufficiency* (Faber & Faber, 1976)
Seymour, John and Girardet, Herbert, *Blueprint for a Green Planet* (Dorling Kindersley 1987)
Sharkey, Olive, *Common Knowledge* (McPhee Gribble Publishers, Melbourne, 1988).
Shephard, Sue *Pickled, Potted and Canned* (Simon and Schuster 2000)

Fifty Tales from the Kitchen Garden

Simons, Arthur, *The Vegetable Growers's Handbook* (Penguin Books, 1945)
Smith, Tim, *The Lost Gardens of Heligan – A Brief History and Guide* (Heligan Gardens Ltd, 1992)
Smit, Tim and McMillan Browse, Philip *The Heligan Vegetable Bible* (Victor Gollanz 1988)
Soper, John *Biodynamic Gardening* (Souvenir Press 1995)
Spencer, Colin, *The Heretic's Feast – A History of Vegetarianism* (Fourth Estate, 1993)
Spurling, Hilary, ed. *Ellinor Fettiplace's Receipt Book: Elizabethan Country House Cooking*, (Viking, 1986)
Steer, William, *Gardening Encyclopaedia* (Spring BoOks)
Strong, Roy, *Royal Gardens* (BBC Books, and Conran Octopus 1992)
Sudell, Richard, *The New Illustrated Gardening Encycolopaedia* (Odhams Press)
Talbot, Rob and Whiteman, Robin *Brother Cadfael's Herb Garden* (Little, Brown 1996)
Taylor, Gordon and Cooper, Guy, *Gardens of Obsession* (Weidenfeld & Nicolson 1999)
Thoreau, Henry David, *Thoreau: Walden and other writings* (Bantam Classic, 1962)
Thunn, Maria and Thunn, Matthias, *The Sowing and Planting Calendar: Working with the stars* (Floris Books 2003)
Tompkins, Peter and Bird, Christopher, *The Secret Life of Plants* (Allen Lane 1975)
Tucker, David M. *Kitchen Gardening in America* (Iowa State University Press, 1993)
Tusser, Thomas *500 Points Of Good Husbandry* (OUP 1984)
White, Gilbert *Garden Kalendar* (Scolar Press, 1975)
Whittell, Giles, *Have Peas Had Their Chips?* (The Times, June 12 2002)

 Bill Laws

Williamson, Tom and Taigel, Anthea, Editors, *Gardens In Norfolk 1550 – 1900* (Centre of East Anglian Studies 1990)
Woodward, Marcus, *Gerard's Herball* (Bracken Books, 1985)
Zuckerman, Larry *The Potato* (Pan 2000)
Adam The Gardener, (Sunday Express publications)
The Victorian Garden Catalogue, (Studio Editions 1995)
Food, Special reports in The Guardian, (May 2003)

Acknowledgements

Thanks to the staff at the Royal Horticultural Society library, especially Jennifer Vine; to staff at the Henry Doubleday Research Association, the National Trust, English Heritage, National Society of Allotments and Leisure Gardeners, The Museum of Garden History, and Floriade in the Netherlands; vegetable gardeners at Hunger Hill, Nottingham and my fellow allotment holders; the villagers of Bucknell and the Watkins family; Julie Lachaud for French translations; Medwyn Williams of Anglesey; and Debbie Rees at Hampton Court.

www.ingramcontent.com/pod-product-compliance
Lightning Source LLC
Chambersburg PA
CBHW071524040426
42452CB00008B/882